THE COUNTERFEIT
LEGEND

Respected Pony League Manager Lives Double Life Robbing Banks

A Memoir Based on a True Story

VICTORIA SUMMERS

ISBN 979-8-88851-769-7 (Paperback)
ISBN 979-8-88851-770-3 (Digital)

Registration Number: TXu 2-366-644

Book Cover by Amnet

Edited by Vanessa Souisa
Edited by Riley Souisa
Edited by Leah Shelp

https://www.thecounterfeitlegend.com

Covenant Books
11661 Hwy 707
Murrells Inlet, SC 29576
www.covenantbooks.com

Acknowledgments

I would like to thank my family for their support and encouragement in writing my story. My daughter, Leanne Souisa; my son, Darin Sioussat; and Annie, who I raised, gave me a reason to be strong and have meaning in my life. I daydreamed of having children and a loving family from a very young age. No matter what life threw at us, we always stayed close, protecting them at all costs and making sure they would never have to go through the abuse or insecurities that I endured.

I am grateful to my talented granddaughter, Vanessa Souisa, for her excellent editing skills. She is familiar with addiction herself and has been sober now for many years—working as a substance abuse counselor helping lost addicts find freedom through God and pursuing her master's degree in clinical counseling.

Thanks to my grandson Riley Souisa for his format editing and his supporting my vision by encouraging me to be the best I can be and not give up.

I am also grateful to Leah Shelp for her editing ability to pull the most out of me and write my story.

And above all, I give thanks to God, as he has always been with me, guiding and loving me. He took this little broken girl and gave me the strength and passion I needed to make a good life for my children and my six grandchildren, Vanessa Souisa, Christopher Sioussat, Riley Souisa, Dawson Souisa, Tyler Sioussat and Jordan Sioussat.

Contents

1

The Bombshell

In 1963, Los Angeles was declared the Bank Robbery Capital of the World. That same year, my father, John Jennings, was arrested and declared one of the biggest armed bank robbers of them all, unbeknownst to my family and me.

I can't tell you how many times my father made us watch the 1960s movie *Oceans 11*. It must have been his favorite, with his idol Frank Sinatra and the Rat Pack dressed in sleek business suits, cooking up the ultimate Las Vegas heist. I used to call out to my dad, "Hey, Danny Ocean, what are you planning now?" Then I'd laugh as I gave him the military salute. He'd wink back at me, his lips spreading in a tightly sealed smile as if he had a secret to keep. I didn't know it at the time, but that movie meant more to him than I realized. He wasn't simply watching actors on a screen. It was more than that; it was aspirational.

Growing up, I lived with a man who led two vastly different lives engulfed in secrets and deception. My family endured the multiple facets of my father's personality, cruelty and dishonesty juxtaposed with fatherly love and affection. Sorting through it all with the buffer of time, I've come to the conclusion that those of us who have suffered abuse can choose to walk one of two paths in life. We can let it take us over, cripple us, haunt us, and spill onto others, ultimately remaining in the darkness. Or we can step into the light. This is the story of how I found the light.

November 4, 1963, was the day that changed my life forever. My seventeenth birthday was nine days away—only eighteen days before President John F. Kennedy was assassinated on November 22.

That evening, I drove home from my surf club meeting with my high school girlfriends. We'd named our club Nereids after the daughters of Nereus, the Old Man of the Sea. The navy-blue sky stretched over us like a canopy as dusk settled over the Topanga Canyon. It grew darker as I drove up the familiar winding road to Mulholland Drive in Woodland Hills, the Beach Boys' "Little Surfer Girl" playing on KFWB radio. As I sang along, I imagined they were singing a love song to me.

I couldn't stop smiling as I pulled up the hill in my 1960 VW Bug. The tinny radio sang out, and the night air whipped back my hair through the open window. I felt calm and happy at that moment. As the song ended, I rounded the corner to our tri-story home.

The first odd thing I noticed was the row of cars lined up in our three-car driveway, making it so that I had to park on the street. I walked up to the house with a sinking feeling, pausing to look through the frosted windowpane in the front doors. Light glowed inside the house, and bodies crowded around the foyer. I could make out the shape of my father's good friend, Clyde Hankins, whom my father called Hank. He stood with his back to the door, his large frame blocking the view into the kitchen. When he turned, an officer's badge glinted off his chest in the yellow lamplight.

It was the first time I'd ever seen Hank in uniform—he worked for the Los Angeles Police Department (LAPD) and was the father of Terry Hankins, a player on my brother Steven's baseball team. It gave me an odd feeling seeing him all dressed in his uniform.

He must have come from work, I thought, slipping through the door. *This is so strange.*

"Hi, Mr. Hankins," I said. "What's going on here?" I moved into the expansive foyer, glancing down the hallway. Several men in business suits were clustered around the entrance to the kitchen. I flipped my long blonde hair back to get a better look at who these people were. No one seemed to notice me standing there—not even

Mr. Hankins. A small ball of panic knotted up behind my ribcage. "Where's my mom?" I called out.

One gentleman placed a hand on my shoulder and ushered me into the kitchen past the men in suits. Before I could protest, he whirled me around to face my mother. "Barbara," the man said. "Your daughter came home."

My mother turned to look at me, tears flowing from her eyes and staining her perfect olive skin. Her auburn hair fell flat against her head, soaked through with sweat. She looked like a worn-out version of herself, fraying at the edges as if she were slowly coming unraveled. Her aquamarine-blue eyes had darkened and grayed and turned red-rimmed from crying.

"Mom, what's happening? Why are all these people here?" I glanced around the room at the faces I didn't recognize. Somehow, I still held on to hope that she would give me the answer I wanted, one that I could comprehend—that could put things back to normal again. I wanted that more than anything.

She stumbled closer and grabbed me by the elbows. "Vicki," she said, her eyes wild, "your father has been arrested for bank robbery!" Her hands trembled as she spoke the words. Her body shook so violently that she had to sit down. We guided her over to the kitchen table, custom-made of white marble with olive-green leather bench seats. At the opposite end, a man sat with a stack of papers fanned out before him. He didn't look up or acknowledge us, even as my mother broke down and cried.

I sat down next to Mom, trying to make sense of what she had told me. I slipped an arm around her hunched shoulders in an effort to try and comfort her. "Mom, did you know about this?" I asked.

She looked up at me with weeping eyes. "No, Vicki. I had no idea. I thought all the money your dad brought home was from his and Paul's insurance agency."

I nodded blankly.

A man in a gray suit and tie stood watching us from the kitchen door. He sauntered over to our end of the table and stuck out a hand. "Detective Sergeant Vance Brasher," he said. When no one took his hand, he reached up to touch his mustache, eyes honing on my mother. "LAPD, Robbery Division. This is my partner, Sergeant Dick Reed." He pointed to the man at the end of the table with the fanned-out papers.

Detective Brasher looked at us for a minute longer, his face falling blank as a wall. In my head, I urged him to say something, wishing for an explanation of this nightmare from *someone*. Over his shoulder, I watched as my younger brother Steven crept up to the kitchen door. I forced a tiny smile for my brother to see, then turned my eye back on Detective Brasher.

"Yes, it's true," he said as if answering a question. His fingers found his mustache again and stayed there. "I arrested John Jennings and his partner Paul Rosenbluth this evening for armed bank robbery. We've been looking for a pair of bank robbers for about eleven months now, and today we finally caught them. LAPD is calling this notorious team 'the Mutt and Jeff Bandits,' or 'the Counter Jumpers.'"

I locked eyes with my brother, who lingered in the doorway. "Steven, did you know about this?" I asked.

He shook his head. "No, but it makes sense, I guess."

Our father had managed Steven's baseball team for years. They'd spent hours together at the field. I wondered if Steven had suspected this—if he'd seen or heard something I hadn't. I walked over to Steven, looking up at him as he slid his long arms around me. He'd grown taller this year, turning from a lanky boy into a handsome teenager. He had locks of wavy brown hair and our mother's blue eyes that sparkled with mischief, and when he smiled, you could still see where he'd chipped his front tooth on the diving board last summer at the neighborhood pool.

I slid out from under my brother's arms. "My god, Steven, Mom kicked him out weeks ago for cheating on her, and now this? Are we ever going to be rid of this guy?"

Steven shook his head. "I don't know, but if this is all true, he'll be in prison for some time."

Under my breath, I sighed. "Finally. An answer to my prayers."

Over the next few days, the story of our father's arrest spread like wildfire through the papers and TV news. Our friends at school, teachers, and Steven's World Series Pony League teammates and their families were all talking about the notorious bank robber, John Kingston Jennings.

Nobody knew the real story of my stepfather but me.

2

Red Flags

My mother, Barbara, met John on a sunny afternoon during the hot month of July in Burbank. She worked as a secretary to a colonel in the Air Force. He was an airport firefighter and seven years younger than her. Mom, Steven, and I lived with my grandparents at the time, along with my older cousin Linda. Their house had become a safe place for Mom after her divorce.

My biological father, Jack, had deserted us some time ago. Over time, I rationalized his desertion as excusable because of the love we received from our close family members. My mother kept us afloat with her excellent job; she was well-educated and beautiful, inside and out.

My mother met Jack in New York during World War II. Mom was secretary to Stanley Kramer, the famous film producer and director. They made recruitment and training films for the United States Army Signal Corps. Jack was in the Army and worked as a film editor. He had a way with film and could run it through his hands with immaculate care and precision.

During my mother's first week of work at Lockheed Aircraft Plant, a young gentleman entered the office in a fireman's suit. At first, she pretended not to notice him, grinding away at her type-writer when his dog ran up to her.

"Her name's Lady," the man said with a grin as my mother reached down to pet his collie.

"You're new here?" Mom asked.

He nodded, his grin taking over his whole face. "I work for the fire department here. I'm John. Are you going to tell me your name?"

"Barbara." She blushed and glanced back down at her typewriter. When she looked up again, he was watching her steadily. His eyes had an intensity to them that made it so she couldn't look away, and she flinched under his gaze. Specks of gold freckled his soft blue eyes under his thick black lashes.

"Barbara," John repeated, still looking at her. "What's your full name, telephone number, and address, Darling?"

"My—what?"

John chuckled to himself, a light, breathy noise. "Just write it on a piece of paper and leave it at your desk."

My mother gaped, unable to tell if he was serious or not. Before she could ask, John turned and left the office, his collie following at his heel. She blinked at the swinging door.

"He'll be back," said her office mate, Marla, with a wink.

My mother shook her head. "Oh, Marla, I wouldn't care. I'm just over a ten-year marriage with kids. No one would be interested in me."

"You're a beautiful girl, Barbara. He's not going to pass you by."

My mother turned back to her desk. For a reason she couldn't name, she picked up a pen and jotted her information onto a scrap of paper torn from a legal pad. A chill spread over her skin, raising the goosebumps on her arms. She glanced over her shoulder at the door in hesitation. Still clutching the paper, she slipped it under her desk calendar that sat like a mat beneath her typewriter.

She exhaled, then slowly stood up from her desk, making her way to the bathroom on shaky legs. She returned a minute later, clear-headed and composed, intending to throw away the paper where she'd written down her information. When she lifted the calendar, the scrap of paper was gone.

I was six years old when I first met John Jennings. Mom took us kids to a bar in Burbank. The room was dark, and behind the bar was a wall of little cubbies. There were presents individually wrapped inside each cubby. My soon-to-be father stood behind the bar, grinning at us. He was six foot three and lean with perfect chestnut-brown hair that he combed back with his fingers. John was not typically handsome, but he displayed a charismatic confidence with his perfect eloquent speech. He smiled at Mom as we sat at the bar. Steven was so young that he needed to sit on my mother's lap.

"Kids, pick out a gift from the wall. Any gift, and it's yours," John said.

"Really?" Steven asked in disbelief. He was about three years old at the time. Mom helped him unwrap the present and pulled out a brand-new baseball. His eyes lit up. "Look, Mom, it's a baseball!"

Shortly after that, John and my mother drove to Tijuana to get married, but they had to wait a year to register the marriage in California. Surprisingly, John was already married to someone else—the woman who owned the bar where he worked. He had kept this detail from my mother. She should have seen this lie as a glaring red flag and broken it off right then. She was smart about everything—except when it came to John.

We all moved into an apartment together in Sherman Oaks near my grandmother's house. One day, Mom sat Steven and me down and said, "Now that I am married to John, I want you both to call him Dad. And you must never speak of your real father, Jack, again."

I didn't mind calling John my father, except for the times when he would drink.

John enrolled in the Los Angeles Police Department Academy. Mom would put Steven and me in the car and pick him up at night after his training. His enrollment did not last long, though. My mother told us the academy had rejected him for lying in his application, but she did not provide us with any details, or maybe she did not want us to know the truth.

By the time I turned nine, we'd lived in more apartments than I could count and were still on the move. John worked for the Yellow Pages in Los Angeles, selling print advertising in the big yellow book. We moved to a nice little house in Pacoima, which meant another new school and a new identity for Steven and me. It was then that Mom decided to change our last name to Jennings.

"I'm going to your new school with you tomorrow to register you as Vicki Jennings and your brother as Steven Jennings, so we will all have the same last name."

"Is he adopting us?" I asked.

"No, but he will be your father now. *Never* say he's your stepfather to anyone—it would hurt his feelings."

In the new house, Steven and I would watch our parents dance from the hallway. Dad loved to listen to music and slow dance with Mom around the living room—especially to Frank Sinatra, Rosemary Clooney, or Tony Bennett. He was very romantic and charming to Mom. She was a beautiful dancer, having taught Hula in Hawaii after graduating from USC. When they danced, he captivated her completely; she would look at him as if under his spell. One minute everyone was happy, dancing, and laughing. The next, he drank himself into a jealous rage.

There is one night in that house I will never forget. As I lay in bed, I listened to my father yelling, accusing my mother of cheating on him. My fingers wrapped tightly around the edge of my comforter, anger boiling up in the pit of my stomach. *She's innocent*, I thought. *He should be the one accused of cheating.* On several occasions, he'd used me as a decoy for his schemes to get out of the house.

"Vicki, let's go for a drive to the store. Come with me," he would say. I knew I had no choice. He pulled up to a house and parked the car on the street. "You stay in the car. I have something to do here. And don't tell your mother about this, you hear?"

I would watch as a woman came to the door, and my father disappeared inside. I never told Mom. I was so afraid of John, and I couldn't go through another night of them fighting. It wouldn't have mattered anyway; she could never refuse his allure.

Later that night, I heard him shout from the living room, "Barbara, you bitch! Who have you been sleeping with?"

I winced at the sound of breaking glass and the thud of a fist hitting my mother's beautiful face.

"No one, John! No one!" she screamed back.

The door to the bedroom flung open, startling me, and in burst John with my mother ahead of him.

"Wake up! Wake up! Kids, look at your mother!" he yelled at Steven and me as we wiped our sleepy eyes, staring at our half-beaten, bloody mom.

He shoved her toward us to ensure we saw her and pulled back her hair to expose her cut lip. Her face was streaked and stained with blood. He let her go, pushing her onto my bed as he left the room to pass out on the couch. She managed to call my grandmother, who picked us all up and took Mom to the hospital. She needed stitches on her lip. They left a scar on her pretty face, a permanent reminder of the brutality she would suffer for years.

Steven and I slept at Grandma's house, where we finally felt safe. In the morning, she took us to the hospital to see Mom, but children weren't allowed in the hospital rooms, so we stayed outside. Grandma opened the window into Mom's room so we could see her in her hospital bed. Her face was black and blue, swollen around her lip and eyes. It was hard to see her in so much pain. I felt so powerless, unable to help her or stop this madness.

"I love you, Mom!" I shouted through the open window. I lifted Steven up to blow kisses, and she blew them back from her hospital bed.

After several days, she left the hospital and joined us at Grandma's house.

"Mom, haven't you had enough?" I begged. *"Please*—don't go back to him, please! You shouldn't make your kids go through this. It's hurtful, Mom!"

It took less than a week for us to cart ourselves back to the Pacoima house, where John greeted us as if nothing had ever happened. My mother's scars were the only thing telling the truth.

3

The Abuse

I never used the word *abuse* to describe my early childhood. As much as I knew in my heart that what John did was wrong, his abuse became normal to me. It wasn't until I had been married for ten years and needed to see a counselor that this idea came to my attention.

"Vicki, do you realize that you were physically and mentally abused by your stepfather?" my counselor asked me.

"Not really," I answered him. "I never put a name to it before. I just thought his cruelty was because of the alcohol. When the drinking stopped, he was a completely different person. Everything went back to normal."

One of the things that became normal in our household was corporal punishment. Dad was a retired Marine who had lied about his age, enlisting at just fifteen years old. Serving at such a young age didn't help him in thinking he was raising military kids. He was so indoctrinated in keeping a clean environment in the military that he continued the practice at home. After our weekly housecleaning chores, Dad put on white gloves and gave an intense inspection, running his gloved hand over the top of the doorjamb molding, checking for dirt invisible to the naked eye. If we failed the test, we were disciplined and sent to bed without dinner.

He always told us, "When you're in the Marines, and they want to show you how to break an arm, they break an arm."

Despite the abuse we endured, my brother and I had some fun times with our dad too. When he ran out of alcohol, we would all march down the street to the local liquor store singing the Marine Corps Hymn. It was quite a sight for everyone watching us, but we enjoyed it.

Dad loved to gamble in Las Vegas, but I don't remember any mention of big wins. He and Mom would take us kids to the casino daycare while they would spend the night playing poker. Other times, Mom would drive the car around with us piled in the back seat until Dad ran out of money. When he finally returned, smelling of smoke and alcohol, he'd say, "Barbara, give me your wedding ring. I'll hock it to get us some food and gas so we can get home." She did, and we all ate bologna sandwiches on the drive.

The first time I flew in an airplane, I was ten years old. I sat wedged between my mother and brother as we flew south to Mexico to pick up my father from the Tijuana jail. He'd been arrested for driving while intoxicated. The police had impounded his car and stolen all of his precious scuba diving equipment from the trunk in the process.

"That jail was *repugnant*—I never want to go through that again!" he said as he walked out of the jail, shoving through the double doors with more force than necessary. His hair was mussed, and his clothes smelled of sweat. I'd never seen him so disheveled. My father always prided himself on his good hygiene and meticulous grooming. The jail was obviously beneath him. "It was so horrible," he went on. "With just a pot in the corner of the jail to do your business in."

Afterward, we made our way to the Tijuana marketplace. The streets were lined with festive, colorful rows of shops, each one crowded with tourists. We stopped in front of a leather store, my father eyeing the display before going inside. He picked up a leather bullwhip from the shelf and unraveled it slowly.

"Man, that's a great feeling whip," he said, swiping it through his fingers. "Look, Vicki. Come and smell the leather." He held the whip up to my nose.

"It does smell nice," I said. "Sort of musky."

It was foolish of me to believe that whip was a souvenir from our shopping spree in Tijuana. That whip became my enemy and the pinnacle of my worst memories. He used it to whip us across our bare legs if we ever displeased him, the sting lasting for hours, sometimes even days. He would make us stand in a corner for hours, maybe all night, without food. I remember standing in the corner and praying to God that this would stop. I couldn't help but wonder why our mother didn't protect her children from this kind of treatment.

John's abuse was not only physically painful but also psychologically damaging. On many nights, he demanded I come and sing for him as he listened to music in the living room. He would yell drunkenly, "Vicki, come in here and sing for me! Come in here, now! Stand in the living room and sing me a song!"

He knew I struggled to carry a tune and would laugh himself silly as I tried to match the notes of the songs. Humiliated, I would sprint away from him, but he would catch up to me easily with his superior size and strength. He would grab me by the hair and throw me, fully clothed, into the ice-cold shower as punishment for trying to get away.

One of my worst and most frightening memories took place in the field behind our house. I had just turned eleven, and Dad had bought himself a BB gun for Christmas. As Mom cooked dinner on the stove, he grabbed his gun from the shelf and called out, "Come on, kids. Let's go outside for some fun."

As Steven and I followed him out back, he yelled for us to "Run as fast as you can! Get out there and run!"

Fearing for our lives, my brother and I sprinted behind old cars and bales of straw as he fired off a round of shots. We darted around the field, breathless and wild-eyed, hiding behind whatever we could find to avoid becoming his moving targets. It was the most frightened I had ever been—we felt like wild animals, hunted and preyed on.

As I reached my preteens, I slowly developed the courage to stand up to my father as I realized I needed to protect my brother from his abuse. I would drive him crazy when I retaliated and shouted, "Stop it! Stop it, now!"

I used to beg my mother to let us go live with Grandma again. I fantasized about the peaceful life that waited for us with her. She was a retired Los Angeles elementary school principal who always helped us with our homework. I finally felt loved in her home, and I wasn't afraid to go to sleep when I was with her.

I thought, *If I could just stay with her for a little while, maybe my family would have peace. Maybe with me gone, there wouldn't be any more tension and conflict.*

Throughout my life, my father had many issues, vices, and addictions. His abuse toward us was only the tip of the iceberg. He was an alcoholic, a con artist, and a compulsive liar, but his greatest addiction was his uncontrollable gambling.

My father would bet on just about anything he could in a desperate attempt for money. He craved the high of winning—poker, sports, and horse races. He even had his own bookie, whom he'd call before the football games. At a horse race with him and my brother, I watched him rip up hundreds of dollars in lost bets. He shrugged his shoulders and winked at us.

"Oh well," he said with a twinkle in his eye, "you win some, you lose some."

Blessed is the man who endures trial, for when he
has stood the test he will receive the crown of life
which God has promised to those who love him.

James 1:12 (RSV)

4

Sober

After years of suffering through a vicious cycle of lies, abuse, drinking, and gambling addiction, my mother finally divorced John. We rented a house in Granada Hills, and I started junior high at yet another school where I didn't know one person—an awful but familiar feeling for me. By that point, I had already enrolled in over ten different elementary schools. I had never had a real life.

On my first day of junior high, I filled out a questionnaire asking about my family life, social events, and even the name of my favorite radio station. The questions shocked me to my core—I couldn't answer any of them. I knew *no* radio stations; I didn't listen to popular music. I had spent so much of my life caring for my mother and brother that I'd never had the luxury of being a kid.

Without John, Mom slowly began doing better and was even dating someone from work. She worked as a civilian secretary to the government at Rocketdyne in Canoga Park. Each night, my prayers ended with, "Dear Lord, please don't let them get back together."

It was an amazingly peaceful year without John in our lives, but I still suffered from nightmares that haunted me each night when I shut my eyes. They were always the same frightening scenario: my stepdad would return to find us, and the cycle would start all over again.

One evening, Mom entered the living room and just stared at Steven and me.

"What?" I asked. "What's wrong, Mom?"

"You two need to get cleaned up and put on some nice clothes," she said. "We're going out."

"Out? Why?" I asked. "Where are we going?"

"Your dad has been sober for one whole year now. They're giving him his cake tonight at the AA clubhouse in Studio City. He wants us all to be there."

"I'm not going!" Steven yelled.

My stomach flipped, but I forced my voice to come out calm. "It's okay, Steven. They're divorced. They won't be getting back together. Right, Mom? You aren't getting back with him? Right?"

She looked at me with hard eyes, her face empty of emotion. I could tell that whatever she was thinking, she was not going to share it with me. "Come on, Vicki," she said. "Give me a break. I just want to see him get his one-year celebration and meet his new friends. He's doing so well. We need to support him."

The AA clubhouse looked like any other house on the street, with worn-down white paint and a sun-bleached roof. There were black shutters on the windows, and the door was open as we climbed the porch steps. The living room had been converted into a large meeting room, with a hundred or so chairs lined up in rows and an aisle down the middle that led to a large wooden podium. The walls were red paneled wood, and fluorescent lights hung from the ceiling. A small elderly woman greeted us by the door with a cigarette dangling from her yellow-stained fingertips. Her aged skin was creased with wrinkles, but when she smiled, you could see her inner glow.

"How can I help you?" she rasped.

"We're here for the meeting to see my husband, John Jennings, get his one-year cake," Mom said proudly.

"Oh yes. John is out on the patio."

"Thank you." Mom nodded.

I stiffened. *There it is*, I thought. *Mom referred to John as her husband again.*

We walked by rows of tables adorned with large silver coffee pots, water jugs, bowls of candy, and a smattering of ashtrays. In the middle of the table was a white frosted sheet cake decorated with a large green shamrock, a long pipe, and one large candle in the center.

"Look, Steven, that must be Dad's cake." I pointed to the table. John was a proud Irishman. "I guess they won't be having any Jameson whiskey tonight," I said under my breath.

Around the corner, a redwood door opened out onto a cement patio. In the center of the patio, my tall father wielded a wooden paddle in front of a large ping-pong table, playing against a stocky man in black-framed glasses. Dad was dressed in his work clothes, a white cotton button-down with rolled-up sleeves, a thin black tie, and matching dress pants. His black loafers were, of course, buffed to a shine.

"Hi, John," Mom said.

He looked at the three of us, set down the paddle, then reached for Mom. He pulled her in and kissed her on the cheek. "I'm glad you're here," he whispered against her ear.

Heat flashed through me and lit up my cheeks. I placed a hand to my red face and swore to myself that I would go live with my grandmother if they got back together.

Mom looked beautiful, as always, in a clingy red knit dress with a slit on the side that showed off her legs in black high heels. Mom was tall, and in heels, she towered at five foot ten. One of the reasons she was so attracted to my father was because of his height. The patio lamplight shimmered against her wavy auburn hair. She used to say with a smile, "Just because you're a redhead doesn't mean you can't wear red or pink."

Steven ran toward John, his face lighting up as John caught him in a hug. "I missed you, Dad."

"I missed you too, son," John said.

I folded my arms, not wanting to cause trouble, but inside, I was fuming.

John turned to face me, straightening up a little. "Hi, Vicki," he said. He cleared his throat. "I'm glad you came. It's a big night for me." He lifted a silver lighter up to a cigarette and inhaled smoke.

The stocky man from the ping-pong table made his way over, adjusting his glasses as he looked at us. "I'm John's friend, Paul

Rosenbluth." We shook hands as he continued to talk. "Your dad has been working hard on the twelve-step program this last year."

"I don't know anything about that," I mumbled. I turned on my heel to head back to the main meeting room. People were flooding into the room now, taking up chairs in the rows of seats. Clouds of smoke dotted the air over their heads. A man's voice came over the loudspeakers, saying, "It's time for everyone to take your seats so we can start the meeting."

Dad shrugged into his suit jacket as he followed me into the main room. The lights dimmed, with one light shining on the podium up front. We took seats about five rows back, with Dad seated next to the aisle.

The speaker announced, "Tonight is a celebration for several members who've completed a milestone in their sobriety. First, we have John Jennings. John, please come forward."

Dad stood up and walked down the aisle to the podium.

The announcer continued, "John, you've gone through amazing changes since you joined AA one year ago today. You go out of your way to help others, you sponsor men, and you are always ready to lend a hand to anyone that asks. Congratulations on your one-year anniversary of sobriety."

The room erupted in applause. John moved up to the podium and cleared his throat. "Ahem. Good evening, and thank you all for coming tonight."

I glanced around the room at the people intently listening to him. He was an excellent public speaker with previous experience as an on-air disc jockey in Minnesota. His voice rang out clear and strong into the room. John was born an only child of high society parents in Saint Paul, Minnesota along the winding Mississippi River. He was well-educated and earned a degree in English from the University of Minnesota.

"I'm incredibly grateful to be a part of AA and work the program to help myself stay sober. I'm so happy that my family is here today—my wife and children. I hope they can see the change in me. Thank you."

As the room applauded again as I wondered what to think. It sure sounded nice, but I knew it was too good to be true. Still, I thought, *What if it is true? What if he has changed? Mom loved him so much…but maybe she's only addicted to his charm.*

We made our way over to the refreshment tables, where a woman stood ready to light the candle on John's cake. Paul appeared at her side, smiling. "Come on, John, blow it out," he said. "If you still have any air left after smoking all those expensive cigars!"

My mother cut the cake, handing Steven and me each a piece. She smiled brightly at John. He leaned over the cake and kissed her on the mouth.

When she pulled away, the look of joy in my mother's eyes melted away some of my anger. Seeing her happy, I wished it could always be this way. Her smile lit up the room. I still distrusted John, but maybe, I thought, just maybe things would be different this time.

On our way out the door, John stopped us to introduce us to some of his friends. "This is Neva," he said, motioning to a woman with dark red hair. Neva was stunningly tall with clear blue eyes. Standing next to Mom, they looked almost like sisters. "And this is her husband, Kelley," John continued. He nodded to the man standing beside Neva, his shiny black hair slicked back against his head. "They have invited us to their home in Studio City next week for dinner."

Steven and I looked up at our mother, who smiled and replied, "It's nice to meet you both. We can make some plans to meet this week."

My father's friend Paul approached us with his wife. "I'd like you to meet my wife, Gaye," he said.

My mother extended her hand. "Oh, Gaye, it's so nice to finally meet you. I hear our husbands are going into the insurance business together."

My heart picked up speed. "Mom, what are you talking about?' I blurted, then lowered my voice. "John is not your *husband.*"

Mom reached over, placed her arm around my shoulder, and leaned down to whisper in my ear. "We'll talk about it later, Victoria Lynn." I could tell she meant for me to drop the subject.

"It's going to be an interesting adventure with these two," Gaye said with a laugh.

"Sure is," Mom agreed. "John is an excellent salesman. And he'll be even better, especially now that he is sober."

Even youths shall faint and be weary, and young
men shall fall exhausted; but they who wait for
the Lord shall renew their strength, they shall
mount up with wings like eagles, they shall run
and not be weary, they shall walk and not faint.

Isaiah 40:30–31 (RSV)

5

The Baseball Legend

Later that same year, Steven took a liking to baseball. He found he had a natural talent as a catcher and a hitter, so he joined the Little League in North Hollywood, and Dad happily supported him. Baseball was something they both enjoyed. Their love for the game grew them closer than ever, and their relationship blossomed as a result. Dad was still attending his AA meetings and spent plenty of time there working through his steps. Paul and Dad opened their insurance agency and became good friends. They both had a gambling addiction in common.

Kelley and Neva, who we met at the AA meeting, became a big part of our lives. They came to all of Steven's baseball games. We spent time at their home, and Mom and Neva became best friends. Neva had a baby grand piano in her living room and could play and sing like an angel. Sometimes she would work with me, trying to get me to carry a tune, but it was always a fruitless effort.

Things were going well between Mom and Dad. Mom seemed happy, and Dad, no longer drinking, made an enormous difference in our home life. He was so busy with work, AA meetings, and baseball that, for the first time, they had nothing to argue about. The year flew by, and then summer was over.

In November 1960, Mom and Dad remarried in Vegas. I had just turned thirteen, and we moved out to Chatsworth in the west end of the San Fernando Valley, out in the sticks. The main street in the area was Devonshire Boulevard, a two-way highway that all the eighteen-wheelers used to drive up on their way through Central California. We were surrounded by horse ranches and orange groves, the smell of both distinguishable from our backyard. It was much different than the city we'd left behind.

Moving was heartbreaking for me, and I had to leave my best friend, Christine, behind. We had been friends since the fourth grade. At that point, I had attended five different junior high schools and would have to make new friends again. Neva and Kelley moved also and bought a house near us in Canoga Park.

Dad purchased a newly invented pitching machine for Steven, giddy with excitement as he set it up outside. All the kids on our block were suddenly drawn to our backyard, hoping for a chance to try it out. The orange groves across the street from our home gave us plenty of room to play ball. I believe this was when Dad got the idea that he would make a good coach—he loved the attention and admiration he received from playing ball with the neighborhood kids.

All the attention soon went to his head. He cut his long, slicked-back hair into an athletic crew cut. He'd always had a passion for baseball. He took us to watch the Hollywood Stars play ball in South Los Angeles at Wrigley Field. In 1958, Los Angeles became the home of the Dodgers. We spent a lot of time there and would eat at Philippe's Deli in downtown Los Angeles. They made the best French dip sandwiches. The waiter would bring a bowl of different relishes and pickles to the table, and all of us would talk and laugh as we ate.

After two years of working together at the insurance agency, John and Paul rented an office on Van Nuys Boulevard in Northridge. They were allegedly so successful that Dad bought us a new home in an affluent area of Woodland Hills on Mulholland Drive, south of Ventura Boulevard.

One night, Dad came home with a surprise present for Mom. We all gathered in the living room as she lifted the lid of a long white box and unfolded the tissue paper inside. She gently pulled out the most gorgeous, two-toned tan mink stole I had ever laid eyes on. She wrapped it around her shoulders and stroked the luxurious fur. It was extravagantly beautiful and soft, with a buttery silk lining.

I started at Canoga Park High School and met some kids that liked to surf, so I thought I would try it too. The location of our new home was an easy drive over the hills to Malibu Beach. I had been asking Dad for a surfboard, and one day he approached me with a secretive smile.

"Vicki," he said. "It's time I bought you that surfboard you've been asking for. Go get ready, and I'll take you over to Val Surf in North Hollywood."

"Oh my gosh, I'm so stoked!" I screamed for joy as I ran up the stairs to get ready.

Once inside the store, Dad talked to the salesman to get the scoop on all the boards. He was clueless about the sport, and I was just starting to learn to ride the waves.

"Okay, Vicki, here's the deal. I'll get you a used board for now, but as soon as you learn to surf, I'll buy you a brand-new custom-made board. How does that sound?"

"That's a deal!" I said with excitement.

The salesman loaded up the nine-foot board into the back of our station wagon. I later discovered it was too long for my liking, but I used it anyway. After I gained some experience, my father followed through with his promise to me. He bought me a brand-new custom board from a local surf shop called Flaherty's in Canoga Park, where all the kids hung out after school. For once in my life, things were seemingly normal; my family was stable, I had stopped moving schools, and I had friends that liked the same things I did—surfing and boys.

When Steven turned thirteen, he advanced to the Canoga Park-Woodland Hills Pony League in baseball. Dad was so excited about this that he volunteered to be the team's manager. This was right up his alley—to be in control. He chose the batting order, starting pitcher, and relief pitchers. He spent all the time he possibly could with those boys. There were countless days when he would leave the office early, dropping everything he could just to get to the practices on time.

I can't remember a time when Dad missed one of Steven's games, and I knew how much it meant to him to be out on that field. It was almost as if he was reliving his own childhood all over again as if he could win the Pony League championship game for himself—his glove in one hand, eyes on the ball, feet digging into the freshly cut grass as a crowd cheered under the bright stadium lights. Being the team manager gave my father the pride and worth he so desperately desired. At the end of each game, win or lose, those boys meant the world to him.

The team played so well that they quickly made All-Stars. They won the district tournament and, later, the sectional tournament. They were soon on their way to National City, California, for the regional game, winning the Western Divisional championship as well. They were undefeated with a 12–0 record. The following day, at 7:30 a.m., they flew to Washington, Pennsylvania, to play in the Twelfth Annual Pony League World Series. Unfortunately, they lost to Evansville, Indiana, and came in second place.

The 1963 Pony League World Series players were fifteen impressive thirteen and fourteen-year-old boys. My brother Steve Jennings, Dan DeSantis, Terry Hankins, Arnie Murillo, Bob Johnson, Larry Yount, Mike Murphy, Bruce Davis, Mike Welcher, Bob Sherwin, Greg Blackburn, Rick Dempsey, Ron Flickinger, Randy Cohen, and Bruce Lockhart made up the Canoga Park-Woodland Hills league.

We greeted the team with a big welcome-home celebration at LAX airport. Mom, Dad, and Steven walked into the terminal with sleepy eyes, carrying their luggage as a marching band played, and all the relatives and fans cheered. A small parade followed, with the families in tow. The motorcade carried the team along Canoga Park Avenue, up Topanga Canyon Boulevard, and ended in the parking lot on Ventura Boulevard.

The Pony League players were all invited to see the LA Dodgers play Houston in a doubleheader at Chavez Ravine. Don Drysdale met with the boys, took pictures with his arm around Steven's shoulder, and shook hands with the star pitcher Randy Cohen. Jim Gilliam congratulated the boys and took pictures with Bobby Sherwin and Bruce Davis.

On September 14, the Canoga Park Elks Lodge hosted a banquet in honor of the team. The boys received trophies, and our local Bank of America manager gave Dad an award for Outstanding Contribution to the Community.

Six of these talented young athletes went on to become professional baseball players. Rick Dempsey played catcher for twenty-four seasons in the major leagues and won World Series MVP honors for the Orioles in 1983. Larry Yount played for the Houston Astros. Bruce Davis, Terry Hankins, Bob Johnson, and Randy Cohen, the star pitcher, all played in the minor leagues. Yount's younger brother, Robin, who attended games as a bat-boy nicknamed "the Kid," went on to play for twenty years for the Milwaukee Brewers. He was named All-Star three times and MVP twice, and in 1999 he was inducted into the Baseball Hall of Fame.

With all our success, I finally felt proud of my family. My father was a successful business owner. I was making friends at school. My mother was happy, and Dad was uncharacteristically attentive to us kids. There wasn't a cloud on the horizon.

"Wow, things really have changed," I told myself.

Trust in the LORD with all your heart, and
do not rely on your own insight.

Proverbs 3:5 (RSV)

6

The Double Life

After the excitement died down, Mom fell ill and ended up in the hospital. Her stress and anxiety had always been high, but now she needed medical help. She called to me in a panic as she stood in the living room, "Vicki! I'm choking!"

My heart raced as I ran in to see about her. "What do you mean, Mom? Choking on what?"

"On my tongue!" She put her hands to her face, trying to relieve the stress.

Her relationship with John had caused her tension and stress to snowball, gradually building until she couldn't bear it anymore. She seemed happy most days on the surface, but beneath her polished exterior, she didn't trust John.

I thought things had been good all this time, but Mom hadn't been telling me everything. In the past, I had always been the one to care for my mother, to comfort her in her physical and mental anguish. This last year, however, I'd gotten a break from my caretaking, both of my parents consumed by the success of Steven's baseball team.

But now she needed me.

I snapped to attention in the living room. "I'm calling your doctor!" I shouted. "You need to get to a hospital now!"

My mother was admitted to the hospital that evening. The next day she called me from her room. "Vicki, are you coming to visit me today?"

"I will later this afternoon. You don't sound good, Mom. What are the doctors saying?"

"I'll tell you when you get here. Please, just hurry!"

I ran a hand across my forehead. "Bob's coming with me. We'll both see you soon."

My boyfriend Bob McDonough and I had been going steady for over a year. We were best friends, and we did everything together. We hopped into my car and headed to the hospital. When we got to Mom's room, I could see she was upset.

The hospital billing had contacted her insurance company, and on the report, they found my dad's name on two separate policies.

"Look," Mom said. "John K. Jennings. But one at a different address than our home on Mulholland Drive." She handed me a slip of paper with an address written on it. "The other address listed is an apartment on Ventura Boulevard in Woodland Hills. Vicki…will you and Bob go check it out for me, please? Find out what's there."

Half an hour later, Bob and I pulled up to the apartment, a two-story building with white stucco walls. We walked through the iron gates to an alcove with gold-plated mailboxes on the walls. I scanned the mailboxes for the apartment number and stopped. There it was, written in little gold letters on the mailbox: my father's name, *John Jennings*.

I took a deep breath. We walked up the stairs to the apartment and knocked on the door. My heart pounded in my chest.

"No one's there," Bob said.

"Let's go to the manager and see if we can get in."

We knocked on the manager's door, and a man in denim overalls poked his head out. I handed him my driver's license. "Sir," I said, "my dad, John Jennings, lives in apartment 223. He asked us to come by to pick up a paper he needs for his job. He's working all the way at his office in Northridge. Can you let us inside?"

The man looked us up and down and nodded. "Sure, but I'll need to come with you folks." He led us back to apartment 223, unlocking the door with a small silver key. Bob and I walked into the living room. It was furnished in a modern style, and in the corner, I could see a record player with a stack of albums. I recognized the albums as the same ones we had at home—exactly my father's taste in music. I felt my face grow hot, trying my best to keep my composure so as not to alert the manager outside. On the kitchen table, I picked up a note in my dad's handwriting: "Darling, see you tonight. Love, John."

My stomach dropped.

The bed was unmade from both sides, and a pair of women's panties were tangled in the sheets. Disgusted, I looked at Bob. "Let's get out of here," I said, my voice coming out hoarse. "I've seen enough."

In the car, we sat in silence for a few minutes as the shock of what I'd just seen washed over me.

"Vicki, you're shaking," Bob pointed out.

I glanced down at my hands and shook my head. "What do I do, Bob? Do I tell Mom the truth? She's already so stressed all the time. I don't want to make it worse."

Bob reached for my hand.

"Don't answer that, actually," I said. I knew telling her was the right thing to do. I had kept things from her before, and it hadn't worked out well.

We went home, and I called her from the house phone. She took the news surprisingly well, almost as if she was relieved. "Well, this makes sense," she said in a firm voice. "Vicki, I have no choice but to ask him to leave."

I wasn't home the day that John moved out. I heard he rented a house in Laurel Canyon, got himself another tri-color collie, and named her Lady—the same name as our dog at home. Mom had the house legally Homesteaded, so the lender could not evict us if she could not make the house payments. The divorce saved my mom from any legal action against her.

After the last year of stability, I had mixed feelings about John leaving. It hurt to think that he could so easily replace us, yet I was also glad he was gone. Maybe now Mom could finally get on with her life and take care of her own mental health and us. But without John, we would have no income.

After all that happened, Mom didn't take John's cheating, double life, or the divorce as well as I had thought. She became so depressed that she went to bed early one night, swallowing an overdose of sleeping pills beforehand. I woke with a niggling feeling at the center of my chest, unable to shake the thought that something was wrong. I decided I had better check on her and made my way to her bedroom, cracking open the door. When I looked inside, I could see that she was out cold. The empty bottle of sleeping pills lay open on the nightstand.

My throat constricted.

"Mom? Mom, wake up!" I yelled. I shook her by the shoulders, but she did not move. My throat clenched. I picked up the phone to call for an ambulance. Fifteen minutes later, we rode together to the hospital. I sat in the waiting room as they pumped her stomach. After what felt like hours, a nurse found me in the waiting room to tell me they had revived her.

I hung my head in my hands and breathed. "Can I see her now?"

The nurse shook her head. "She's not awake at the moment. It may be a few hours before she's ready to speak to anyone."

Mom stayed in the hospital for a week, trying to build up the strength to carry on, but the roller coaster ride was just beginning.

A month after Dad moved out, Mom received a call from the Los Angeles Police Department informing her that Dad had been arrested. They'd caught him on another drunk driving charge, and after five years of sobriety, he'd gone back to drinking. He was set to appear in court on November 17. Upon hearing the news, I went to my bedroom to be alone and stayed there for a while. My normal, stable life had been ripped straight from my fingers as if it had never existed.

No temptation has overtaken you that is not
common to man. God is faithful, and he will not
let you be tempted beyond your strength, but
with the temptation will also provide the way of
escape, that you may be able to endure it.

1 Corinthians 10:13 (RSV)

7

The Bank Robber

On November 5, the front page of the *Los Angeles Herald Examiner* read in big, bold-print letters:

BANK HOLDUP SPREE BUSINESSMEN "DOUBLE IN CRIME" NABBED
Pair Got $111,218 in 13 Stickups.
BANK "COUNTER-JUMPING" BANDITS VIRTUALLY LEAPED INTO ARMS OF THE LAW

It was heartbreaking to watch my normal life disappear in one short day, but I was resilient in my effort to keep our family together. Besides, I was used to the fact that my life was unstable, and I knew my angels were protecting me.

Mom, Steven, and I watched the evening news, where we found out most of the details about the robberies.

LAPD had branded John and Paul "the Mutt and Jeff Bandits" after a long-running cartoon comic strip because of their height; John towered at six foot three, while Paul was a stocky five foot seven. In the comic strip, Mutt was very tall, and Jeff was very short. Others called them the "Counter Jumpers" because Paul would jump over the counters and scoop up all the money into a large canvas bag while my father kept the tellers distracted.

Dad and Paul would stake out the banks for several weeks prior to the robberies. They would watch carefully from a distance at local restaurants, doughnut shops, or sometimes from the street in their parked cars. They would monitor the time of day when the armored trucks arrived to pick up the money, making sure when they made their move, there was plenty of cash left to steal.

During the robberies, they wore dark-blue business suits, pin-striped ties, and black-tinted sunglasses. My dad always took his sunglasses off for any baseball photos so nobody would be able to identify him.

They would enter the banks calmly. Dad would stand at the front door and announce to the room, "We beg your indulgence; we will only take forty-five seconds, and no one will be hurt."

Then Paul jumped over the waist-high entry door with a gun in one hand and a bag in the other. He'd scoop up all the money that each teller had in their drawer.

The first robbery happened on January 14, 1963. The two bandits used a .22 caliber rifle and a BB gun (likely the same gun he used to shoot at me and Steven outside). By the seventh robbery, they upgraded to a .38 caliber revolver and a .38 semiautomatic rifle. They never shot a gun or physically hurt anyone. The pair robbed thirteen banks in eleven months and stole more than $150,000.

Counter-Jumpers' Robberies			
Count 1	January 14	Bank of America, Sylmar	$8,572 Cash
Count 2	January 29	Bank of America, Northridge	$11,217 Cash
Count 3	February 25	Bank of America, Encino	$2,436 Cash
Count 4	March 22	Citizens National Bank, Reseda	$3,659 Cash
Count 5	April 5	Bank of America, Van Nuys	$9,759 Cash
Count 6	May 8	First Western Bank, Woodland Hills	$8,035 Cash
Count 7	June 12	United California Bank, Los Angeles	$3,679 Cash

Count 8	July 1	Bank of America, Anaheim	$25,482 Total: $16,821 Cash $7,718 Checks $943 Credits
Count 9	July 22	Bank of America, Burbank	$27,685 Total: $6,599 Cash $21,086 Checks
Count 10	August 6	Bank of America, Pasadena	$5,525 Cash
Count 11	September 11	Bank of America, Culver City	$11,352 Cash 25 Blank Money Orders
Count 12	October 18	Bank of America, Gardena	$13,238 Cash
Count 13*	November 4	Bank of America, Panorama City	$20,373 Cash

*The myth of the number 13 being unlucky came true for these bandits.

The day before each bank heist, my dad and Paul would purchase an old junker car for about a hundred dollars from a private party. On November 4, my dad drove the getaway car, following Paul in his own vehicle out to a residential neighborhood several miles from the Panorama City Bank of America. They left Paul's car and drove together in the junker to Van Nuys Boulevard, passing by the coral brick Bank of America. They parked the junker car along a tree-lined street and waited silently, preparing themselves physically and mentally as they cased the area. Then they grabbed their canvas sacks, straightened their ties, and took a big gulp.

With sunglasses on, they entered the bank. John announced the robbery as usual, while Paul jumped over the counter and scooped up the money. It went fast and easy. Fifteen minutes later, they walked casually onto the street and got in the junker car. They transferred the money from their tote sacks into their leather briefcases, then drove back to where they left Paul's car.

It was easy for Paul to stay calm during an adrenaline rush. He was a retired Marine, stocky but agile. Paul would laugh in amusement as he jumped the chain-link fence, showing off on his way to where they'd left his car.

Unfortunately for them, a man noticed the strange sight while watering his lawn; two men in business suits and sunglasses climbing out of a beat-up car and jumping a chain-link fence. The man noted Paul's license plate number, repeating it to himself as he ran into his home. He scribbled down the number and dialed the operator, asking to be connected to the police immediately.

The police decided to investigate the suspicious activity because the description fit the profile of the two bank robbers from just twenty minutes earlier. When they ran the license plate, they discovered it was registered to Paul's wife, Gaye. They showed up at Gaye's house in Sylmar, where they demanded at gunpoint to know Paul's whereabouts. In a panic, Gaye called her husband as police officers monitored the call. Paul responded that he was working in the Northridge office. The officers stayed with Gaye, still holding her at gunpoint, while the detectives left to investigate.

When the task force burst through the door, they found Paul and my dad with guns and rifles laid across the table. All of the money from that day's robbery was stuffed into waste baskets and spread all over the floor. FBI agent Ken Arnold handcuffed and arrested them.

> Thirteen individual indictments were submitted to the grand jury. Between January 14, 1963, to November 4, 1963, in Los Angeles County, within the Central Division of the Southern District of California, defendants *Paul J. Rosenbluth* and *John Kingston Jennings*, by force and violence and by intimidation, knowingly and willfully took from thirteen banks and thirty different tellers money belonging to and in the care, custody, control, management, and possession of thirteen national banks and members of the Federal Reserve System and banks whose deposits were insured by the Federal Deposit Insurance Corporation.

> In committing the offense heretofore charged, defendants *Paul J. Rosenbluth* and *John Kingston Jennings* assaulted and put in jeopardy the lives of thirty tellers and hundreds of patrons using a .38 revolver and a .38 automatic: dangerous weapons and devices.

The sentencing was scheduled for December 19 in Los Angeles US District Court. I didn't get much sleep that night and the day was cloudy and cold. We made good time driving to the courtroom from Woodland Hills, but it was nerve-racking not knowing what to expect.

Mom, Steven, and I waited in the hallway outside the courtroom. I remember the dress I wore, black with a white collar. Mom's leg bounced against the bench beside me. I caught sight of Dad coming down the hallway in an orange jumpsuit. A large chain linked him to several other men, all with their hands and feet constrained in handcuffs. Uniformed guards led the men into the courtroom, with Mom, Steven, and me filing in behind.

The judge read the charges against Dad, thirteen counts of bank robbery. John and Paul each pleaded guilty. Judge Thurmond Clarke gave them each a reduced sentence because they were so cooperative with the investigation. The court ordered counts 1 through 6 of the indictments to be dismissed; they were sentenced to five years on counts 7 and 8 to run consecutively and five years on counts 9, 10, 11, 12, and 13 to run concurrently, totaling ten years.

Dad was sentenced to federal prison at the McNeil Island Correction Center in Washington State. Paul was sentenced to the Federal Correctional Institution in Lompoc, California. They both sent letters to the judge pleading for leniency due to their family's hardship.

Cast all your anxieties on him, for he cares about you.

1 Peter 5:7 (RSV)

8

Aftermath

The last six months of high school were rough on me emotionally. I stayed away from school as much as possible and avoided my friends. I was so embarrassed knowing that people were talking about my dad. I later found out that several boys at school were protecting me from cruel comments. I'll never forget you, Mike Frost, Dick Jeffrey, and George Boskovich, my high school heroes.

Without John's income, we weren't able to stay in our beautiful home in Woodland Hills, so we moved into an apartment. As I walked across the football field at my graduation, a weight lifted off my shoulders. Knowing I would never have to see anyone from my high school again filled me with deep-seated relief. I could start over, become a new version of myself if I wanted to, and most importantly, extract myself from my family's past. As soon as summer was over, I got a job at a retail store in Van Nuys. I made new friends and avoided anything and anyone that knew me or my story. I never shared the truth about my childhood or my dad's criminal past with anyone.

As a graduation present, my grandmother bought me a car for one hundred dollars from a woman she knew in her retirement community. For the first time in my life, I finally felt free. It was like I was coming up for air after holding my breath for months. I spent my days working and my nights going out with my new friends. I reveled in the new life I had created for myself, but it felt precarious as if it could be wrenched away from me at a moment's notice.

To my confusion, my new life upset Mom. She grew angry and bitter toward me, though I didn't understand why. Maybe it hurt seeing me move on when she couldn't, or maybe she felt left behind. But after weeks of fighting, she told me it was time I moved out. She watched from the doorway as I gathered my things, piling them mindlessly into my car. Before I left, she held out a hand.

"What?" I asked.

"Give me your key."

I stared at her, then reached into my pocket and placed the key to our apartment in her hand. I had no place to go, so I slept in the backseat of my car and showered at my girlfriend's house before work.

The new year brought with it a seasonal cut in jobs, and I was let go from the retail store. Homeless and jobless, my cousin Linda took pity on me and took me into her home with her husband and two babies. I fell in love with her girls, Janine Anne and Kristin Lee, I later named my daughter, Leeanne, after them. I got a job at Bob's Big Boy, the famous hamburger restaurant on Lankershim Boulevard in North Hollywood where I met my husband, who was also named John. We got married on June 30, 1967, in Las Vegas, Nevada, and started our life together. It was the Summer of Love.

Steven was never the same after Dad's arrest. We talked about the robberies and jail, but he did not want to talk about his feelings with me. I remember him going into his room and closing the door, in hopes of being left alone. He continued to play baseball during his senior year of high school, but he did not earn a varsity letter as he had before; he did not meet the school standards, either academically or he didn't perform satisfactorily to his past level. Without Dad, his heart wasn't in it, and he never recovered emotionally or physically.

Later that year, the doctor diagnosed Steven with lumbar spine degeneration from a traumatic injury when he was playing baseball at about fourteen years old, which ended his baseball career.

On November 5, 1968, Steven was drafted into the Vietnam war at nineteen years old. He began his basic training at Fort Ord in

Northern California. Steven had an exceedingly tough time adjusting to basic training, so much so that he began to contemplate suicide. After three weeks at camp, he was granted emergency leave to visit our mother in the hospital. She was recovering from surgery from a previous injury.

I'm going home to die, Steven thought as he boarded the bus home. *I'm going to end this suffering.*

On the second day of his leave, Steven swallowed forty-five of Mom's sodium amytal sleeping tablets. Mom had come home from the hospital to find Steven unconscious, and he was immediately admitted to the Veterans Affairs Hospital. He had to be there for three weeks, on involuntary admittance, so they could monitor him. After discharge he was sent to Fort MacArthur in San Pedro, California for processing, then he was released to duty and given twenty-four hours to find his own way back to Fort Ord. Instead, he went back to Mom's apartment and tried everything to get into a hospital so he would not have to return to basic training. He called his commanding officer, his doctor, and a lawyer. None of this resulted in his hospitalization. So Steven never returned to Fort Ord and was classified as AWOL (absent without leave) for over six months. His mounting anxiety and fear that the Army would come after him made him paranoid, but they never did. In June, he turned himself in and was sent back to Fort Ord to complete basic training. After four days he was so anxious, tense, and depressed at camp, that he was allowed to go home for a few days. He never returned to complete his training.

Steven lived with Mom and her dog Suzette in a two-bedroom apartment and remained AWOL for another two and a half months. During that time, he began making concrete plans to end his own life. One night in late October, he fasted for twenty-four hours and then took forty Seconals, a sedative-hypnotic drug, at about eleven o'clock. Mom was away that night and wouldn't be returning until the next day. I had to go to work at Lockheed and was pregnant with my first child at the time. I was nauseous that day, so I left work early and went home to rest. I called Mom's apartment and became worried when nobody answered. I had a bad feeling about Steven.

Something told me I should investigate, so I took my spare key and walked over to the apartment.

When I opened the door to Steven's room, I saw him lying on the bed asleep. Candles flickered all around the room, giving off an eerie glow. My skin went cold. I knew immediately what was happening—I'd seen it before with Mom. I bent down at his side, checked his pulse, and felt his heart still beating. Frantic, I called the police. Steven was taken to the local hospital where he was treated intensively for several days before regaining consciousness. The administration contacted the military, who came in and handcuffed him to the bed.

Steven fell into a coma and was transferred to the VA hospital in Brentwood. He had developed aspiration pneumonia from his long period of unconsciousness. Upon his recovery, he was transferred to Letterman General Hospital in Granada Hills on Oct 31, 1969, for evaluation.

The doctor diagnosed Steven with an "inadequate personality, chronic, severe, manifested by a long history of maladaptive behavior and poor response to social and military demands." I'm sure this came from the traumatic event of our dad's arrest, which Steven witnessed at fourteen years old. He did not have a psychiatric disorder, so he could not be discharged through regular medical channels. Although, the doctors strongly recommended that he separate from the service through the administrative office. He stayed at Mom's apartment until the Army officially settled terms with him.

Dad had been in prison at McNeil Island in Washington for a few years when they discovered he had cancer in his tongue. They split his tongue down the middle, removing half of the cancerous side. It made it difficult for him to talk and be understood. When I heard this news, I thought, *He can't con anyone now with his charming words*. He was then transferred to the Federal Correctional Prison in San Pedro, California. It was about a forty-five-minute drive from North Hollywood, so Mom visited him as much as she could.

One day Steven and I decided to go with Mom to visit Dad, mostly out of curiosity. The prison buildings were surrounded on all sides by a chain link fence, with spiraling barbed wire on top. The American flag rippled from atop a tall metal pole, next to the lettering "Federal Correctional Institution, Terminal Island, California," and a big round sign read "Department of Justice – Federal Bureau of Prisons." As we walked through the courtyard, I looked up at the tower to my right and noticed the guards standing with rifles. We waited patiently inside while Mom showed her ID and gave our information to the guard.

We entered through a massive, steel electric door, which locked with a click behind us. An armed guard escorted us down the hall to a large open room with picnic tables and benches. He directed us to a table and instructed us that we were not to have any physical contact with our father. We had to sit across the table from him at all times.

Apparently, Dad and Mom had communicated prior to our visit for her to bring some of her valium pills to the prison and give them to him. I saw her put a bunch of the pills in a piece of tinfoil when we were still in the car. I didn't understand what she was doing until I saw her put the wrapped-up foil in her mouth. When she kissed dad, she passed them to him in his mouth. Dad wanted to sell the pills to other inmates to buy food or use instead of money when he was playing poker.

My leg shook as we waited. I hadn't seen my father for nearly five years. I was nervous and jumpy. It was the first time I had ever been inside a prison.

Dad sat down across the table from us. "It's good to see you, Vicki. And you, Steven. I've ordered a leather belt and two leather wallets custom-made by the inmates. I'll get those mailed off as soon as they're finished."

"Thanks, Dad, for thinking of us," I replied as I scanned the room where other families were visiting.

He sent me a card that year for my birthday. Inside he had written out a message:

> Sweetheart—I am sorry this cannot be more. If
> all goes well, you will have a sweater from me
> in the near future, after Mom gets hers. For the
> present though, I am so thankful you are alright.
> You are a wonderful young lady, and John is a

very lucky young man. I wish you the happiest of birthdays and the very best of everything.

Happy birthday, sweetheart. Love, Dad.

During the last year of his incarceration, Dad was placed on a work-release program and made some money on the job. He worked at a retail store near the prison. The guards drove him to work each day and brought him back to the prison. He stole merchandise from the store and sold it to the inmates. I remember thinking, *He really is a thief at heart.*

In January 1970, Dad was released early from prison for good behavior. He served seven years of his ten-year sentence. Upon getting out, he was able to hire an attorney for Steven and pay for him to get a medical discharge from the Army with full medical benefits. He mentioned that Steven had messed up his life, and he wanted to help him. I thought, *Maybe he should take some accountability for Steven's problems, but then again how long do you blame your parents for your mess-ups?*

On February 19, 1970, at the Hollywood Presbyterian Hospital, I gave birth to my first child, a beautiful little girl named Leanne. She had dark brown curly hair and brown eyes like her daddy. The next day, after very little sleep, my mom and dad came to visit me together. It was the first time I had seen Dad since his release from prison. I was happy to see them, and thankful Mom would finally be happy. Shortly after, Neva and Kelley walked in. They had remained good friends with Mom through the years John spent in prison.

Neva handed me a present. "I hope you like it," she said as I opened the gift.

I lifted up a pink, hand-crocheted baby blanket for Leanne. "Did you make this, Neva?" I asked. "Can you teach me how to make these?"

"Of course I can," Neva replied with a smile. Neva's baby blanket started a tradition for me of hand-crocheting blankets for all my grandchildren.

After I came home from the hospital with Leanne, I found out that Mom and Dad had moved into an apartment some distance from me. I found this odd, when they could have moved into the apartment next door. Grandma was still helping them get on their feet and pay their rent. She had even bought them a used car. For a while, all was good. It was nice to get a break from the drama since I was a new mom.

Several months passed, and I was remarkably busy with Leanne. My maternity leave was over, and soon I went back to work at Lockheed. Leanne was in childcare at a loving, private home. It was a struggle to keep up with my husband working full time at Lockheed in a Flight Line Mechanic apprenticeship program and attending school at night. One evening, as I spoke to Mom on the phone, I got the feeling that something was wrong. Her voice was hoarse and quiet; she avoided my questions or changed the subject. I knew she wasn't telling me the truth about how things were between her and Dad. She didn't want to worry me because I was so busy. I decided to go check out the apartment and find out what was really going on.

I drove over to the complex and took my baby Leanne with me. It was a terribly run-down, low-income area. My heart clenched, thinking of her living in this environment after all she had been through. I knew she'd thought everything would be better again when John got out of jail.

I knocked on the door and waited. When she answered, I could tell she was a wreck, as she nervously stroked her tiny black poodle, Suzette.

"Mom, how is everything going?" I asked. I took a seat on the couch and set the baby carrier at my feet, Leanne asleep inside.

"Not good, Vicki." My mother pulled nervously at her sleeves. "John is worse than before he went into prison. He's drinking again and taking pills… You know how he gets when he drinks."

I nodded. "Mom, you've been drinking and taking Valium, too, for years now. You waited all this time for him to change…to be the husband you've wanted, but all this time it's been destroying you."

For years, I'd watched her wait for him to get out of prison, writing letters to communicate, while she patiently stood by his side. My mother had wholeheartedly believed John would change, but it consequently destroyed her each time he didn't. Each time, he returned to a life of substances and abuse, she suffered for it. And now she needed my help to get away from him. I knew she wasn't strong enough to do it on her own.

"I have a baby now," I said slowly. I glanced down at my sleeping daughter, her tiny eyelids fluttering at the sound of my voice. "I have to take care of her first, and I need to get back to work. But, Mom…I'm willing to take you to the hospital if you'll let me. You can finally get off the pills and get away from John." I set my jaw. "Will you go with me? Please?"

When she looked up at me, a defeated, broken expression darkened her features. Her blue eyes were veiny and red from lack of sleep. She was clearly exhausted, her shoulders hunched where she sat on the opposite end of the couch. For a moment, she was quiet. Then she whispered, "I'm not sure what to do."

I felt a pull in my chest. I didn't want to leave her this way. I worried about what would happen if she didn't get help, but I couldn't force her to go with me; I had my own responsibilities at home now. I couldn't be her caregiver anymore.

"John will be home any minute now," she said, glancing over her shoulder at the door. "He has something to talk to me about. I don't know what it is, but it sounded serious."

Reluctantly, I pulled myself up from the couch and lifted the baby carrier onto my arm. It hurt me to leave her there with John, but I didn't have another choice. I told her I loved her and left with Leanne. The next day, I called several times to check that she was okay.

There was no answer.

For we have not a high priest who is unable to
sympathize with our weaknesses, but one who in every
respect has been tempted as we are, yet without sin.
Let us then with confidence draw near to the throne of grace,
that we may receive mercy and find
grace to help in time of need.

Hebrews 4:15–16 (RSV)

9

The Addiction

Later that night, I received an unexpected phone call. My husband John answered.

"Hello? Is Vicki Sioussat there? I'm Elizabeth, and I'm calling about her mother, Barbara Jennings. This is Camarillo State Hospital."

John looked into my eyes with sadness as he handed me the phone. "It's the hospital. About your mom."

Mom had been admitted to the Camarillo State Hospital for depression and substance abuse. Neva and my father had brought her in. After asking a few questions, the receptionist informed me that I would be able to visit Mom the following week. I asked the lady if she knew anything about my mom's dog, and she told me that John and Neva had taken the dog with them and that my mom was upset and crying.

"Can you give her a message from me?" I asked. "Tell her I'll be there next week and to hang in there and I love her."

I turned to my husband, and we stared at each other. He didn't say a thing, just shook his head. Both of us had grown up in an alcoholic home and were used to the cycle of addiction. Still, it didn't make it any less difficult.

My mother spent six months in the hospital healing, although the doctors continued to give her Valium and Librium for her anxiety and alcohol withdrawal. She was chemically dependent on the drugs.

My husband and I bought a little yellow house with white trim on Wish Avenue in Van Nuys, California. I loved our new street name; it reminded me that dreams come true. Mom moved in with the three of us, my husband, Leanne, and me. We made a space for her in our large family room, where she slept on the fold-out couch. We did our best to make her comfortable there, hoping she would stay until she got back on her feet. Mom got a job in aerospace again, but she was older this time. She had no car and was forced to endure a two-hour long bus ride to El Segundo each day. Riding the bus began to take a toll on her and soon became too much, so she quit her job. Because of a pre-existing back injury, she qualified for Supplemental Security Income (SSI), disability, and housing. As a government employee all her life, she did not get social security benefits. She rented an apartment a few miles from our home, and we got her settled into her new place.

Dad had left Mom for Neva, her best friend, and taken her dog, Suzette, with them. Mom spoke of this often and was very resentful about it. Missing Suzette was so hard for Mom that she got another black toy poodle puppy and named her Tiki. After waiting all those years for John, she was brokenhearted that he had left her. She found out that Neva had been secretly visiting John in prison ever since he was moved to San Pedro, and they may have planned this for a year. It seemed a calculated maneuver to stay with Mom during his time in prison, so the parole board viewed him as rehabilitated and honest. Neva had plenty of money after her divorce from Kelley and after selling the house in Canoga Park. My mother was furious that they had all been together in the hospital room when Leanne was born. I didn't tell her that I was happy John had gone on to another woman. I hoped it would finally sink in that he was a selfish liar who used those around him for his own personal gain.

The timing was good for Mom to get her own place. My family needed a break, and I now had my second child, Darin, who was born on Christmas Day 1972. I wanted to take care of my husband and kids with no drama or dysfunction. Plus, I met a young girl, Annie, through my cousin Linda. She had been abandoned by her parents and needed a home, so my husband and I took her in to live with us. She was shy at first. It took me about a year to get her to trust me and become a part of our family. Leanne and Darin were so gracious and loving toward Annie becoming their big sister. Apparently, when you can't help your parents, you reach out and help someone that wants it.

Steven had moved down to Redondo Beach with a girl he had met. He was supporting himself by singing and playing his guitar on the pier along with handyman work and cabinetry. The laid-back beach culture embraced Steven's musical style, hippie image, long curly hair, and infectious smile. He smoked marijuana and fell in love with the contemporary folk music of Bob Dylan, Donavan, and Joan Baez. Steven was a pacifist at heart; one reason why he hadn't fit into his military role. This genre of musicians, with their protest songs, fit his personality and beliefs. One summer, he took his guitar and a backpack and hitchhiked up to San Francisco to witness the peace and love movement he desired, only to find it was fake. He was severely beaten and robbed on his way to Haight and Ashbury Street, so he returned home to the Southern California beaches and reclaimed his role as a street musician.

The late 1960s and 1970s had a rise in the epidemic of illegal drugs, where people enjoyed listening to psychedelic music while high. I do not know what came first with Steven, but he was now addicted to pain meds. Doctors gave him prescriptions for his back pain, due to his lumbar spine degeneration from his traumatic injury. Doctors prescribed him a mix of sedative and hypnotic sleep drugs, as well as opioids: Tylenol with codeine, Valium, Placidyl, and Darvon. Most of these drugs are no longer obtainable today due to their highly addictive properties.

It became a battle to keep Steven away from Mom. He was down on his luck, living on the street with no food or drugs, and would crash at her apartment most nights. I refused to let him come to my home. I didn't want my kids around the lifestyle of a drug abuser. Both he and Mom had developed addictions to Valium, and he made a habit of stealing her pills. She would phone me late at night, saying, "Vicki, Steven has taken all my pills, and I must have them! Can you drive me to urgent care? Please, Vicki! I'll die if I don't have them tonight!"

I could hear the panic in her voice. "Mom, I have the kids with me, and they're getting ready for bed. They have school tomorrow, and I have to work. Can't it wait?"

"No, it can't wait! I have to get them tonight!"

I wanted to say no to her, but, for some reason, I couldn't. Despite my other responsibilities, I took her to the hospital to get her pills. She could easily manipulate me—I had been her caretaker for so long. She was my mother, after all. How could I say no to her?

Things grew worse with Mom, and I begged her repeatedly to get help or go to rehab. It was not easy to get into a hospital, especially without money. I would call every day to see if there was a bed available, and when a space opened up, she would have to get there right away to be admitted before the bed was taken. I finally got the news that a bed had opened up in a hospital in Van Nuys.

I called my mother to tell her about the available bed at the rehab center. I told her to pack her bags right away, bring her Bible, and that I would be there in thirty minutes to pick her up.

"Okay, Vicki, I can do this," she said.

When I arrived at her apartment, Mom seemed nervous; she was jittery and wide-eyed, glancing around the room. She stood in the kitchen, clutching the handle of her bag with white knuckles. Despite her nervousness, she was packed and ready to go, so I felt relieved.

As we walked through the hospital, traipsing down long, white halls saturated with the sterile smell of rubbing alcohol and disinfectant. We passed the many doors, each with two beds and two people per room. At the front desk, we filled out her admission paperwork and spoke to the medical staff. Everyone seemed helpful and kind. Once her intake was complete, I grabbed her by the hands and prayed for her. When she opened her eyes, I pulled her into a big hug.

"I love you, Mom," I whispered into her ear. "I'm so proud of you for doing this."

When she pulled away from me, tears flecked her cheeks. She shook her head, her voice low and pinched in her throat. "Vicki…I don't want to do this…"

"I'll call the nurses every day to check on you, Mom. I *promise*. I know it will all be okay. Trust me." I squeezed her shoulders. "I'll see you in a week."

I had parked my car across the street from the rehab facility, and I sat in the front seat for some time, reflecting and praying. As soon as I turned the key in the ignition, about to drive away, I saw the faint shape of my mother in my rearview mirror. I blinked, swiped the tears from my eyes, and sat up straighter. The figure came out through the side door of the rehab center and walked with a bowed head to the bus stop. I brought a hand to my mouth. *No*, I thought. *No, it can't be her*. I watched as the figure sat down on the bench, setting a paisley bag down on her lap. I had watched my mother clutch that same bag this morning—it was definitely her. She sat there for maybe twenty minutes until the bus arrived with a screech. Then, as if it were any other day, she climbed onto the bus. I watched the bus doors swing shut behind her as something like a fist balled up in my throat.

I called my mother that night to ask her why she had left rehab. She gave me a long list of excuses, many of which didn't make any sense. She told me that she had feared for her safety as soon as I'd left and that she believed the medical staff would try and kill her if she stayed. Again and again, she begged me to not be upset. I told her I loved her and that I was not upset, but disappointed. When I hung up the phone, I sat there at the end of my bed and stared at the blank wall. Then I got up, and made my children dinner.

That was the last time I tried to get my mother's help. I often asked myself if I was the one enabling her, but she was an adult and still addicted to her pills—and to John. I did not want to be an enabler or be responsible for her continued addictions, but she was over fifty now, unable to work, and had been through hell and back. For years now, she had been drinking and taking Valium just to get through the day. The doctors had put her on an oxygen machine because she had developed emphysema and a heart condition. Even still, she continued to smoke cigarettes in-between breathing oxygen from the hose hooked up to her tank. I couldn't think about this too much—imagining that one day the tank would explode from the heat of her cigarettes. It was a struggle not to worry constantly. All I could do was pray for her; I had to turn her over to God and let go of my worries. Because of this, I didn't visit her much; it was too hard on me emotionally to see her and Steven living together in an apartment, feeding off of each other's addictions.

During this time, I struggled in my own life, trying to keep my marriage together while raising three kids. My husband, John's, drinking was growing out of control. He was a good man and very loved by our children, but he was also a high-functioning alcoholic (though nothing compared to the severity of my father). I believe I rationalized my husband's drinking as okay because of the addiction I had grown up around. I didn't think it would ever spiral out of control.

John drank every night throughout the entire marriage. He either stopped at a bar after work, staying for hours or came home and drank until he passed out on the couch. I was very lonely and the dreams I had once had for my family on Wish Avenue were shattered by alcoholism again. In my heart, I knew there had to be more to life than what I had experienced so far.

John and I threw a party at the house one weekend. We invited our friends for rock and roll music, food, drinks, beer, shots, and dancing. When people drink, they tend to talk and tell stories: some get loud and obnoxious, but some are sentimental. I remember standing in the kitchen as a friend of mine asked to share with me about her Christian faith. I had always believed in God, but I never knew much about Him. Still, I had always felt that he was protecting me through the years—things could have been so much worse. There were times I thought I wouldn't make it out of it, and I knew that something else had pulled me through. So, as we drank our wine, I listened to her tell me about how Jesus loved me. I did some research on my own, in hopes of finding the answers I had been looking for. Slowly, I surrendered to the idea and became a believer. My faith not only helped me with eventually forgiving my parents, but it saved my marriage for seven more years.

Unfortunately, my husband John did not feel the same way. He wanted to keep his drinking and the bar lifestyle more than he wanted to accept Jesus into his life. In his mind, he felt that I was the one who had changed in the marriage. I did change, but for the better. I continued to stay in the marriage because I believed God would be able to reach his heart and change him too. But he never changed; we finally divorced after fourteen years of marriage and were able to remain friends.

Have no anxiety about anything, but in everything
by prayer and supplication with thanksgiving let
your requests be made known to God. And the
peace of God, which passes all understanding, will
keep your hearts and your minds in Christ Jesus.

Philippians 4:6–7 (RSV)

10

The Encounter

Several years later, I remarried very quickly to my new husband, Terry. In October 1981, we decided to take a weekend excursion to Catalina Island, twenty-six miles off the Southern California coast, in celebration of our marriage. Boarding the *SS Catalina: The Great White Steamer,* I was filled with anxious excitement. Salty air whipped my face as we waited on the dock to board. I had never been on an ocean-going boat before, and the thought of that, combined with the possibility of seeing my father, made me nervous. I had heard that he was living on Catalina Island with Neva, his now wife. After ten years of separation, we would be in proximity again.

"Terry, do you think I should call my dad when we get to the island?" I asked.

He squeezed my hand, looking down at me with his crystal-blue, caring eyes. "Vicki, let's see how you feel when we get over there, okay?" He winked at me and gave me a dimpled smile.

Over the loudspeaker, a voice instructed us to stow all our bags in the middle of the boat between two yellow ropes. The ship was packed, but we found two seats on the outside upper deck.

The dock was swarming with seagulls, and I watched their curiosity and their graceful wings as they glided from one piling to another. One seagull perched close to us and stared at me, shaking its head back and forth as if warning me, *No!*

As we pulled out of the port, the sky turned misty and gray, covered by an eerie fog. The boat pulled away from the dock and cruised smoothly out of the harbor onto the open sea. I could see the whitecaps and feel the saltwater splash onto the deck, spraying my arms and giving me chills up my back.

The gray haze was lifting, and ahead I could see Catalina Island from the bow of the boat. The sun shone golden on the island and Avalon Harbor was packed tight with boats and lots of activity.

The captain announced, "We will be docking in about fifteen minutes," as he sounded the horns, signaling to the hands on the dock to get ready.

After we grabbed our luggage and walked onto the dock, I felt the warmth from the sun on my face. Avalon Harbor was on the sunny side of Catalina Island. We headed toward the center of town. The small beach area was already crowded with tons of sunbathers. I could hear children laughing while playing in the water, and it made me smile. The mesquite BBQ smell flowed over the harbor from the docked boats. The smell made us hungry, so we decided to stop for lunch.

We walked farther down Main Street to the famous green pier. I stepped on the wooden planks and noticed some boards were loose.

"Be careful," Terry said as he took my hand. "Come on, let's go back to Main Street and find a place to eat."

We walked down the street and went to a large open center filled with tour buses. The sign read *GUIDED TOURS*, going into the interior of the island. There was a phone booth right in front of me on the sidewalk. I glanced at Terry and shrugged. "I think I'm going to check out that phone book and see if my dad's number is listed."

Terry nodded as I made my way to the booth, thumbing through the dense book. When I found the name Jennings, my heart picked up speed.

"Look! Terry, his number is in the book. I'm going to call him. We can eat after. Do you have some change?" He handed me a few coins, and I picked up the receiver, put the coins into their slots, and dialed the number.

"Hello."

I recognized my father's voice and cleared my throat. With a shaky voice I said, "Hey Dad, it's Vicki. I'm out here vacationing on the island with my husband, Terry. I was wondering if you would like to see me?" There was a moment of silence.

"Where are you now?" he asked.

I glanced up at the street signs. "At the phone booth at the tour center on Catalina Avenue."

"Wait there, Vicki. I'll be right over."

I hung up the phone and turned to Terry, "He's coming to meet us now!"

Terry and I met through my best friend, Chris. We fell in love very quickly, and it was a romance I was starving for. He had never been married before and was seven years younger than me. He had no children of his own and openly accepted my children along with me. We spent many evenings talking about our past, and he knew all about my abusive childhood and the history of the man I was about to see.

I thought, *Why am I doing this? What is wrong with me? Am I trying to stir something up?* I was so curious about John's new life and how he might have reinvented himself again. I wanted to see if he was living a double life here on the island. I thought, *Does anyone know who he really is? Does he ever think about me and Steven?* There were so many questions running through my head.

Standing next to the phone booth, I could see him coming down the street. I hardly recognized him anymore. He wore faded blue jeans and a black windbreaker over a yellow turtleneck. His white boating hat was pulled down to cover his ears. His hair, full beard, and mustache had turned reddish in color, bleached from the sun. His tan face was weathered and aged.

"Surprise!" I laughed nervously as he opened his arms to hug me. It felt strange but familiar to hug my dad again.

When we pulled apart, I stepped back, pointing at Terry. "Dad, this is my new husband, Terry."

He turned to Terry and shook his hand. "Nice to meet you. I heard about you from Vicki's mother."

I stepped back. "You've talked to Mom? What? When?" My eyes darted from John to Terry. I tried not to show how shocked I was to hear this.

"Yes, we have talked, mostly about your brother. He needs money all the time. She told me about your divorce from John and that you remarried."

Dad asked us both to lunch. Neva would join us later, after her shift as a tour guide at the Casino ended.

We ate at a small seafood restaurant with an outdoor deck overlooking the harbor. We sat in plastic chairs on the dock as seagulls circled above us in the sky. After we'd eaten, Dad told us all about what he and Neva had been doing over the last ten years. Neva and my father had gotten married and bought a forty-two-foot trimaran boat, which they'd lived on for a few years. They would dock at the Marina Cortez, Harbor Island in San Diego, but sail it up and down the California coast. They'd named her "the *Good Life*," and it sounded like it truly was. When Neva's mom had gotten ill, they sold their boat to buy a two-unit house here on Catalina Avenue. Dad and Neva lived upstairs while Neva's crippled mother lived downstairs where they could take care of her. Dad worked as a shore boat operator, taking passengers back and forth from ship to shore. Unfortunately, he had gotten skin cancer, so they changed him to the night shift. He had to take all the drunks back to their boats when the bars closed.

As John elaborated on all of his new adventures with Neva, I could feel my face flush hot with anger. I didn't want to hear any more about how good his life was—while he had been out sailing with Neva on his new boat, Steven and Mom were still suffering because of the things he'd done. I tried to listen as best as I could, waiting for him to finish his stories, but he continued on and on. I finally blurted out, "You know, Dad, we never talked much about the bank robberies when you got out of prison. I had so many questions to ask you."

"Shoot, I'll tell you anything," he said.

It was a little hard to understand him, as his eloquent, clear voice had been muffled by the cancer surgery, which had removed half his tongue on one side.

I leaned forward in my chair, scanning his calm face. "Well, first off, why…um…*why* did you do it? I thought you and Paul had a successful insurance agency and were making lots of money. Why would you want to rob banks?"

He nodded slowly. "Paul and I *did* start out successfully, but we did some heavy gambling that left us with no money. It was the first week of January 1963, a new year, for us to get on our feet. We were at the office going over the payments due at the office along with our houses. Paul was worried about not having any money coming in to pay the bills this month. I asked him what he thought we should do. I suggested we go to Vegas and try to win some money back to make the payments that were due. Jokingly, Paul suggested robbing a bank to get the money. And…I guess I didn't think that was such a bad idea, so that's how it started, Vicki." He stopped, glancing down to avoid looking into my eyes.

I thought after listening to his story, *Nobody thought it was a good idea or a joke, especially with a loaded gun.*

He continued, "We planned our first robbery at the Bank of America in Sylmar, right near Paul's house. Maybe at first, it was scary, but then it got easier over time. We just had to keep going— especially after Mom and I bought that new home on Mulholland Drive. I was financially in over my head, and I was just too lazy to work. I wanted to spend all my time with the baseball team." He shrugged.

I folded my hands in front of my face to hide my expression. This was a lot for me to mentally process at the time, but I had to get a few more questions answered while I had him here in front of me. I asked him if the guns they used in the robberies were loaded. He told me they weren't. At the time, I wanted to believe him, but years later when talking with Paul, he said they were, in fact, loaded.

"What was the hardest part of robbing banks?" I asked.

"The hardest part…was right before, putting your hand on the door handle and opening the door to step out of the car. Once you step out that door, you are committed—no turning back."

"I heard on the news that a lady had a heart attack during a robbery. What about that, Dad?" I asked.

"Yeah, Vicki, that was bad. I never wanted to hurt anyone. Thank God she didn't die." His shaky answer was followed by silence. "By the way, Vicki, you know all the money the newspapers reported we stole from the banks was overexaggerated."

"Guess you never thought about the damage you caused." I was shocked to hear the words come out of my mouth. I had always been able to hide my resentments toward him, but now I was opening like a floodgate.

Before he could say anything, Neva walked up to our table, saving me from an embarrassing conversation. "Vicki!" She reached for me, and I stood to hug her. "It's so good to see you, dear, you look great." Neva's hair had turned white. Her skin was tan, and her eyes were still aqua-blue. She retained her classy, sophisticated look, even wearing a nylon windbreaker and stretchy polyester jeans. I thought that she and Mom were aging in the same way, their radiant red hair now bright white. As she sat down, I noticed her pick up her knee and move it into place, pain flitting across her face from the movement.

I had no resentment toward Neva. She had been a big part of my life since I was a young girl. I was almost relieved when she took off with my father. The way they had gone about it was wrong, leaving my mother while she was at her worst. I knew it was painful for Mom at the time, but I wanted John out of her life. She was addicted to him in the same way she was to the pills. At the time, I thought the only way she would get better was if he left her permanently. In my innocent thinking, that would end the addiction Mom had for this man. Of course, it never ended. Even now, they were still speaking.

"Neva, this is Terry, my husband. Did you hear that John and I divorced, and I remarried?"

"Yes, I did. I just want you to be happy, Vicki," she said. Neva was never one to censor her words. She was always brutally honest but still loving.

We spent the rest of lunch updating each other on our lives. I told Neva all about Terry and talked to her about my divorce from John. I explained how great Terry was with my children. Leanne was now eleven years old, and Darin was almost nine and loved to play baseball. I wanted Neva to know about Annie, the young girl I helped raise who was now working for Lockheed and going to college. I knew Neva would like her.

Neva asked me about Steven and informed me that they had been sending him money from time to time, but that was the only contact they had with him. I told Neva I was planning another trip with my children and would love for her to meet the kids. She finished the conversation with an offer to take us on a tour of the island, followed by a glass-bottom boat trip the next day.

I was relieved when the trip ended, and we were back on the ship heading toward home. We had a fun time seeing the sites, and it is a beautiful island, but reliving my feelings of anger and hurt toward my father had emotionally drained me. I was so glad to have Terry with me, supporting my decision to take the chance and face my past. I knew I had been reserved and a bit closed off while listening to my dad's stories.

We never spoke about the reason my father left my mother or the time she had spent suffering in his absence. I didn't bring it up, knowing they would have excuses and defenses on why they'd deserted my mother. They would justify their betrayal because of their love for each other. I did not want to hear anything negative about my mother. It was too painful for me to have anyone put her down; even in her suffering, she was still beautiful to me.

That day in Catalina was the beginning of a new journey in my life. I never told Mom that Terry and I went to the island to see Dad and Neva. It would have only broken her heart to know. I had not known that Mom had been talking to Dad all these years. He would call her from the pay phone on the pier at night after his shift and profess his love for her, even though he was married to Neva. Even after all this time, he could not let her be. He kept her hanging onto that small glimmer of hope.

But the fruit of the Spirit is love, joy, peace, patience,
kindness, goodness, faithfulness, gentleness,
self-control; against such there is no law.

Galatians 5:22–23 (RSV)

11

The New Life and Lies

My mom and Neva both lived a fantasy that John was their soulmate, and they held onto that feeling until the day they died.

One day, Mom called me on the phone. "Vicki, your dad called last night. He's coming to the mainland next week for a doctor's appointment at the VA hospital."

"Is he okay?" I asked.

"It's just a routine checkup," she said. "But he wants to come to your house and have lunch with us. Is that okay with you?"

I paused, unsure if it was. "I guess so," I said slowly. "It's all so unexpected…what are you doing talking to him, Mom?"

"Vicki, relax. I have no expectations. It's been so long since I've seen him anyway—ten years, at least. You know he calls me off and on to chat. He still loves me."

Dad rented a car, picked Mom up, and brought her to my house. It was uncomfortable for me to see them together. I felt so nervous that I hardly touched my food. I was careful not to mention I had seen Dad and Neva back in October, on our vacation to Catalina. I loved both Neva and my mom. I wanted both of them to be happy.

Later that week, my family made the trip to the island to visit Dad. Terry and I, along with my best friend Christine, rented a big house close to Dad's and Neva's house. Christine brought her three daughters, Niki, Raquel, and Shelley. My kids, Leanne, Darin, and Annie really liked Neva, and she was easily picking up the grandmother role. They liked the idea of having grandparents who lived on the island that they could visit anytime. It was a different life over there, slower and more relaxed. The locals were familiar with John and Neva and showed them respect. We always received special treatment anywhere we went on the island.

Neva told me privately that John had a challenging time with his drinking and gambling for a few years after he was released from prison. His drinking inflamed and enlarged his liver so severely that, at one point, he had to be medically evacuated by helicopter to the mainland hospital to save his life. After that was resolved, he managed to stop drinking but started smoking pot and cigars instead.

Neva learned early on to restrict the amount of money John spent on gambling. Dad had started a monthly high-stakes poker game and played right off the pier opening by Main Street. Locals and mainland gamblers came to play every month. Once his monthly gambling budget was gone, he couldn't play or spend any more until the next month. Neva was firm about his limits with money.

My dad had become a member of the Freemasonry Society, a brotherhood of men required to uphold good and moral character. Their values are based on integrity, honesty, fairness, and kindness. Masonry's teachings are morality, charity, and obedience to the law of the land. He had held many positions, working his way up the ladder and becoming the Worshipful Master, the highest office in his Masonic lodge. He would be installed again for his second term as Worshipful Master, and I was invited to the ceremony.

It was a chilly night in January 1983. I stayed at Dad and Neva's home on a covered patio that faced the street with a fold-out couch that I slept on. Across the street was a white country-style church, and its pointed steeple had a big, white cross at the top. At night, a flood light from the street brightly shone on the cross, causing it to glow. Looking out at the cross from my bed, I smiled and said aloud, "Thank you, God, for always being there for me."

The next morning, Dad wore a black tuxedo with a large material envelope hanging from a silky white rope around his neck. Neva wore a shimmery, emerald-green dress, and I dressed in a black, knee-length gown and a jacket with rhinestones. I loved the bling.

The installation ceremony was very formal, with white silk tablecloths and expensive flower arrangements at the center of every table. I soon realized that no one on the island knew about my dad's history. My presence even surprised the locals—they hadn't even known that John had a daughter. One gentleman was so impressed with Dad that he turned to me with a wink and said, "You must be so proud of your father for all the work he did with the prison inmates, counseling them?" I had no reply. I just shook my head and smiled.

John left his past criminal record behind him and allegedly became a responsible part of the community. Once again, he had somehow reinvented himself to become respected by the brotherhood and island locals.

Neva was an Eastern Star, the female fraternity of the Masons. She was involved in many charity groups, including the women's club, and sang at the local Christian church and animal rights organizations. Her heart was pure, with an honest intent to help others.

The next morning, Dad told me, "Let's ride in the golf cart. I'll take you over to the golf course and up the mountain."

"Okay," I said. "Sounds nice."

We went over to the golf course and ate breakfast at the outdoor patio cafe. The first tee was on one side of the street, and it was a long drive across the street to get to the first green. Dad had become quite the golfer since living on the island.

Once we reached the top of the road, we stepped out of the golf cart and looked over Avalon Harbor. The water was still and cornflower blue under a clear open sky. It was a breathtaking sight. I wanted to say so many things to him, but most of it was behind me, so far in the past by now. I had forgiven my dad as Christ had forgiven me. My Christian faith and relationship with God had saved me from crippling anger and the need for retaliation. It gave me peace until this moment in time.

Dad turned to me as the wind picked up and looked me over. His eyes softened. "Aren't you proud of me, Vicki, and how well I've done?"

My heart dropped. A flash of heat shot through my body. My hands and feet prickled and went numb. Hearing him ask this and wanting my approval devastated me because I could not give it to him. I couldn't speak, unable to put words to the feeling that rushed through me as my heart raced against my ribs. It was the most painful question anyone has ever asked me. My mind flashed back to the images from my childhood—of Steven and me darting behind old cars and bales of straw in the field behind our house; standing in the corner while my stomach growled, empty; shivering under a cold shower as hot tears streaked my face. All of it because of him, and all of it for what? Why did it happen at all? And how could he ask me this now, after everything?

My mother's aged face appeared in my thoughts, with her scars both inside and out. Then came the memories of my brother as a young boy, trying to win the affection of this selfish, unimpressible man.

I felt the anger rise in my soul, paralyzing me momentarily. After reliving all of my emotions and disappointments, I couldn't help the resentment that rose up inside of me. It was *always* about *him*, even though *I* was the one to pick up the pieces after his selfishness left us broken.

The wind tousled my hair. I stared down at my feet as the seconds ticked by, unable to look him in the eye. I wished, instead, that he had put his arms around me and told me he was *sorry*. Sorry for hurting me. Sorry for all of the harm he had caused. I wanted him to tell me that he was proud of the woman I had become under the challenging and painful circumstances. I knew in my heart that I would not hear those words. I would have to heal and let go of this. I could not continue to relive it over and over again, or it would break me.

A few minutes passed, but still, the words would not come. All these years, I had been so trained not to speak up to him, which only ever got me punished as a girl. Even now as an adult, I was still so afraid of this man.

After a few minutes, we climbed into the golf cart and headed back, riding up the rolling green hills in silence. It would have made no difference if I had told him of the pain I felt. At that moment, I knew he had no capacity to understand or empathize with me, my brother, or my mother. The damage was already done anyway.

My brother Steven was the one who suffered the most, never coming to terms with his life or his physical and mental pain. For almost a year, I had picked my brother up and drove him to his appointments at Rancho Los Amigos Medical Center once per week. Since his last suicide attempt, Steven had been seeing a physician and counselor for a year now. I wanted desperately to help him stay off drugs and alcohol. From the outside, he seemed to slowly learn how to function again. He took his prescribed antidepressants and anti-panic medications. He rented a room, paid his bills, and did his best to maintain a healthy lifestyle. I helped him shop for groceries when I could. But on the inside, Steven was still suffering.

In his third and final attempt, Steven ended his own life. On September 21, 1995, he jumped off the Santa Monica cliffs by the pier at Ocean Avenue onto Pacific Coast Highway. He was forty-six years old.

When I got back his olive-green puffy parka jacket from the coroner, I put my shaking hand into the pocket and pulled out a raffle ticket Steven had bought that same day from a local Santa Monica church. Folding the ticket in my fingers, I wrapped myself around the jacket as tears soaked the sleeve. It still smelled like him. An ache the size of a canyon opened up in my chest. I stood clutching the jacket and breathing in the last traces of my brother's scent. I wished he would have come to me—why didn't he come to me when I tried so desperately to help him? We could have figured it out together. I could have found a way to help.

Steven's suicide tore my heart in half. I felt so helpless. It gave me a sense of peace to know that he reached out to God before making the final leap.

Repay no one evil for evil but take thought for what is noble in the sight of all. If possible, so far as it depends upon you, live peaceably with all. Beloved, never avenge yourselves, but leave it to the wrath of God; for it is written, "Vengeance is mine, I will repay, says the Lord."

Romans 12:17–19 (RSV)

12

Goodbye Lies

It was midsummer in 1985 when I got a call from Neva informing me that she had bad news about my father. He had been diagnosed with esophageal and lung cancer. She was terribly upset as she explained his diagnosis through sniffling and tears. She told me that Dad was out in the harbor with some guys on a boat last month, and someone had challenged him to jump off the boat's mast. Of course, he asked how much money they would pay him if he did it. The bet was made, and he jumped off the mast. When he hit the water, the blow dislodged a tumor in his throat. Neva had him medically evacuated by helicopter to the veteran's hospital in Long Beach for testing. Neva said that he was at home now but that he would have to return to the hospital for radiation and chemotherapy next week. I told her I would like to see him and that I would be praying for him.

I waited a few weeks to visit my dad in the hospital while he finished his last round of radiation treatment. I called him the night before and told him I was coming to see him. When I got to the VA hospital and found him in his room, he was wearing a hospital gown, and I could tell that he was embarrassed.

"Vicki." He gave me a weak smile, his face looking even more weathered than the last time I'd seen him. "I'll put on a robe and slippers and meet you in the lounge," he said.

"Okay, Dad." I nodded.

I found the lounge down the hall from his room and sat on a large, brown vinyl chair to wait for him. I could see him coming down the long hallway, walking slower than his usual pace. When he finally made it to me, I stood up to hug him. His tall body was visibly thinner, my arms wrapping all the way around him with room to spare. When he pulled away, I noticed his eyes were cloudy, and I could tell he was in low spirits.

"Being in the hospital is terribly humiliating," he said, shaking his head. "It's embarrassing for me, Vicki. This isn't how I like to live."

"How is the pain in your throat?" I asked. "It's so red, it looks raw."

"Well, that hasn't been fun. I'm tired, and the nausea and vomiting are constant. Chemo makes you sick all the time…and *weak*. Vicki, if they don't get the cancer this time around, I won't do this again."

"Well, let's just wait and see what happens before you make any final decisions," I said.

"You know the thing that really sucks?" He said, leaning in. "My golf game was just getting good!" He shook his head and smiled. He was such a proud man, and this experience was wearing on him.

My father knew my strong Christian beliefs, and I had tried to talk to him about the Lord before, but he never wanted to hear it. I thought I would take one more bold shot at it.

I had always been afraid to talk to my dad about my feelings—just as I had been the last time we were together. I'd been unable to bring up my anger about the childhood abuse. Now, it was just as difficult to share about my belief in Jesus as we sat in the hospital lobby. I worried it might upset him.

He sat with his legs crossed, one slipper dangling from his foot. I watched him as his eyes scanned the room and felt the words stick in my throat. I remembered times as a young girl when we'd sit down at the dinner table as a family. Like any teenager, I'd prattle off stories about my friends and me at school or details about my day. Dad would take his steel dinner knife and slap it across my fingers—his way of warning me to stop talking. The memory still stung.

"Dad," I said slowly, wringing my hands. I took a deep breath as he turned to face me. "Remember when I was a kid, and I begged you to take me to church? You let Mom take me and Steven to that Lutheran Church on Sherman Way in Van Nuys."

He gave a half smile and nodded.

I reached for my purse and pulled out a small paper card from one of the pockets. "Look at this little green Easter card I made for you at Sunday school. I had cut out the cross on white construction paper and glued it to the front with these little white lilies, and I wrote, 'To Daddy, From Vicki.'"

He reached out gingerly and took the card, holding it in his hands a minute before finally opening it. As he looked at the bright crayon-colored picture of a family leaving the church, he read the words out loud. "The Lord has risen. Luke 24:34. I love you, Daddy." His eyes welled with tears that spilled over onto his cheeks. "Vicki…I can't believe you would save this card for all these years."

"I know," I said. "I don't even know why I did…"

As he handed back the card, I thought how I had never seen him show emotion before. It was an odd sight. I thought to myself, *does he really have a heart? Or is it the drugs they're giving him for the pain?*

"Well, Dad. I must have had a thirst for God at a young age, and I always felt I had angels protecting me. I never did much about my search until after I was married with two kids, but then I accepted Christ as my savior and became a Christian. I want to tell you about my journey…are you okay with that?" I braced myself and waited.

He gave a half-hearted shrug. "Sure, Vicki. But I usually let Neva take care of the religious stuff."

"That doesn't work with God, Dad. It's just between you and him." I told him about the party I'd thrown with my ex-husband, John, and standing in the kitchen as my friend shared her faith with me. "It was the first time I'd heard someone talk that way about Jesus," I said. "I thought, 'Wow, I had never heard those words before, even as a kid in Sunday school.' So I decided to find out more about it. I called my cousin Linda, who was just as curious as I was about

Jesus, and together we found a church, took our kids and went every Sunday for months. You remember Linda, don't you?"

"Of course, I do," he said. "I walked her down the aisle when she got married."

"That's right. You did. Dad," I laughed, "Linda and I enrolled in Christianity 101 classes at the church. I remember sitting in those classes, listening to their conversations, giggling, and feeling embarrassed. They were so foreign to me, but the information I was learning was what I needed deep down to heal my soul. So, I embraced it. Especially when I started to hear about the love of God and forgiveness." I took a deep breath.

"Dad, back in those days, they had an 'altar call' after the sermon. The pastor would ask anyone that wanted to accept Jesus as their savior to come forward. Linda and I would be in tears at the end of each sermon. But there was one specific Sunday when we looked at each other in a way where we knew we had both been touched by God. Nodding in agreement, we decided to walk to the altar, got on our knees, and prayed together. We asked God to forgive our sins and invited Him into our lives. It was a life-changing moment for me. I knew in my heart that this was God's plan for me and that he had been watching over me all these years. I knew I was supposed to teach my children about Him."

Dad looked away, clasping his hands together in front of him. "I'm glad for you, Vicki. I just don't think God would want me."

"Dad, I know it may feel that way with everything you've done. And you feel shame and guilt for the mistakes you've made in your life, but God forgives us if we acknowledge our sins. He doesn't hold them against us anymore—he wants you, Dad. He wants you because he loves you."

He was silent for a moment, breathing slowly. Then he gave me a gentle smile. "Vicki, I'm tired now and want to go back to my room. Thanks for coming to see me. I love you."

It was the first time I had ever heard him say those words to me. "Wait, Dad, I need to tell you one more thing." I reached for his hand and looked him in the eye. "I forgive you."

He turned away, and I watched him walk down the hall back to his room. I knew that day that forgiving him was for my own peace—not his. In his mind, he had done nothing wrong, or at least he would not admit it to me. That was the last time I saw my dad.

Dad's cancer did come back, and just like he said, he would not continue with further treatment. So he opted out of chemo, and on January 31, 1986, he passed away in the ambulance on the way to the Avalon Hospital.

One week later, off the beautiful California coast on Catalina Island, there was a Friday evening Rosary service for him at St. Catherine's Catholic Church. His Grand Masonic memorial service was held the next day at the Community Congregational Church. At least two hundred people attended the service. He was well known and respected in the Masons, serving as worshipful master for two terms. The Catalina Express ship brought in dozens of his Mason brothers and his professional gambling buddies to say farewell and honor him. I went to the funeral to support Neva. She was all alone now, and I still loved her as family.

Everyone spoke so highly of him and his contributions to society. They praised him for counseling prison inmates, using the knowledge he acquired from his PhD in physiology from the University of Minnesota.

One of his friends stood at the pulpit and shared about his achievements as the Canoga Park-Woodland Hills Pony League Baseball team manager, who'd taken fifteen exceptional boys to the World Series in 1963 and came in second place. Many of his teammates went on to have successful professional baseball careers due to his encouragement and belief in them. His friend told us about an awards banquet that was given in the team's honor, including a presentation from Bank of America, where they gave him an award plaque for Outstanding Contribution to the Community.

A man holding a folded American flag spoke about his service in the United States Marines, serving in Southeast Asia as a second lieutenant. After being wounded in combat, he spent two years in the naval hospital in Long Beach, California. He was awarded a Purple

Heart for being wounded in battle. After his speech, the man handed the flag to Neva.

He was commended for his commitment and dedication to his local Mason lodge, his competitive nature for poker and golf, and his love for Neva and their dogs.

It was difficult hearing all the praise about this man who had lived a double life, reinventing himself over and over again in order to hide his criminal past and abusive behavior.

Not one person at that ceremony knew the truth about John Jennings like I did; all the secrets I kept to myself through the years about him burned inside of me. Not even my mother nor Neva knew who he really was.

He never had a PhD in physiology. He had a Master of Arts in English.

He never worked in prisons to counsel inmates. His years spent in prison were due to his own incarceration for the thirteen accounts of armed bank robbery.

He was never an outstanding citizen as the manager of the pony league. He was part of a notorious duo of bank robbers known as the Mutt and Jeff Bandits, as well as the Counter Jumpers, who evaded capture in an eleven-month robbery spree.

He was never a second lieutenant in the Marines. He was a private first class with an honorable discharge.

He was never wounded in Southeast Asia and spent two years in the naval hospital. He won his precious, valuable Purple Heart in a high-stakes back-room poker game.

He was never faithful to any woman. He was a liar and a cheat.

He never knew how to love or have empathy for others. He lacked moral sense and guilt and was unable to change his behavior after punishment.

He was not just a competitive poker player. He had a serious gambling addiction.

He never cared about the brotherhood. He only cared about the praise and acclamation he received because of his intense egocentrism and superiority complex.

He never did the AA Twelve Steps program. He stopped at number 8: "Make a list of all the persons you have harmed and become willing to make amends to them all." He simply loved being a part of the group so he could gain a reputation and status in the community.

That is why I call my dad John Kingston Jennings,

the Counterfeit Legend

> *Counterfeit.* "Made in exact imitation of something valuable or important with the intention to deceive or defraud."

For God so loved the world that he gave his only
Son, that whoever believes in him should not
perish but have eternal life. For God sent the Son
into the world, not to condemn the world, but
that the world might be saved through him.

John 3:16–17 (RSV)

Epilogue

Forgiveness is a difficult feeling to acquire and maintain. I was born with a naturally forgiving disposition, a behavior I learned at a young age. I was forced to learn how to survive and cope in my abusive home.

I made the choice to forgive my parents, and it brought peace to my soul. I had a whole life ahead of me, and I did not want to hold onto the pain, feel sorry for myself, or be a victim anymore. I hid my trauma and never told anyone about my childhood for fear of judgment. I always strived to create an image of well-being, and it worked. Once, someone said to me, "My, Vicki, you are such a happy person. You must have had a good childhood."

Forgiveness did not take away my memories nor excuse my parent's abuse, but it did heal me and take away my anger and resentment. Forgiveness allowed me not to carry a grudge or dwell on my past.

I hid my insecurities and my trust issues deep within me. I had a tough time believing in people. I always assumed they were like my father in that they were not who they presented themselves to be. Unfortunately, many times I was right.

Growing up, I had no role model for a father. When I became a Christian, it was difficult for me to embrace the fact that I had a heavenly father who I could trust—one who loved me unconditionally.

For most of my life, I was a codependent caretaker for my mother, which started from an early age. I saw this pattern continue throughout my life. I was always trying to rescue and save others because I wasn't able to save my family growing up.

I was overly sensitive to criticism, and it cut me like a knife. It affected me most when others commented on my children, or my parenting style being too laid back.

I panicked when I heard people fight. Loud voices and noises scared me, and I was easily startled and on guard. I lived my life always expecting something terrible to happen.

What I am telling you now, no one knew. I had it all under control, or so I thought.

I give glory to God for giving me the gift of forgiveness, helping me heal from a life of fear and survival, and giving me the strength and courage to face my past so I could live freely to trust and love others as Christ so loved me.

Let all bitterness and wrath and anger and clamor
and slander be put away from you, with all malice,
and be kind to one another, tenderhearted, forgiving
one another, as God in Christ forgave you.

Ephesians 4:31–32 (RSV)

About the Author

Victoria Summers grew up in California's San Fernando Valley in the sixties. She attended the Los Angeles Valley College for Liberal Arts and began her creative journey painting special effects by hand for Hanna-Barbera animation studios. She then moved on to a career in radio advertising and began writing scripts to help market her clients. Now, as a published author, Summers writes about her life growing up with an abusive stepfather, who lived a double life of crime and public admiration. This is her inspiring story of overcoming trauma through her faith.

> See that you do not despise one of these little ones; for I tell you that in heaven their angels always behold the face of my Father who is in heaven. (Matthew 18:10 RSV)